Notes to My Becca

A Father's Thoughts on Welcoming His Long-Awaited Child

C. Stephen Fouquet

Fairview Press
Minneapolis

Published by Fairview Press, 2450 Riverside Avenue South, Minneapolis, MN 55454

Library of Congress Cataloging-in-Publication Data

Fouquet, C. Stephen
    Notes to my Becca : a father's thoughts on welcoming his long-awaited child / by C. Stephen Fouquet.
        p.   cm.
ISBN 0-925190-40-3
1. Fatherhood.   2. Father and Child   I. Title.
HQ756.F68   1995
306.874'2--dc20   95-6540
                                            CIP

First Printing: March 1995

Printed in the United States of America
99 98 97 96 95   7   6   5   4   3   2   1

Cover design: Circus Design
Internal design: Marti Naughton

Publisher's Note: Fairview Press publishes books and other materials related to the subjects of physical health, mental health, chemical dependency, and other family issues. Its publications, including *Notes to My Becca* do not necessarily reflect the philosophy of Fairview Hospital and Healthcare Services or their treatment programs.

The paper used in this publication meets the minimum requirements of American National Standard for Information Sciences—Permanence of Paper for Printed Library Materials, ANSI Z329.48-1984.

CONTENTS

For BLDF and TRDF: Inspiration. Reward.

ACKNOWLEDGMENTS

Several of the poems contained within this book have appeared in the following magazines:

Abbey

Green Zero

Stuff: The Microzine of Miscellany

Zuzu's Petals Quarterly

James River Review

Tight

Notes to My Becca is the result of emotional turmoil and growth — as a child and adult. I thank all at Fairview Press for publishing this book, of course, and I thank you for purchasing it. I also thank the relatives and friends who populate these pages. Without their understanding and misunderstanding, support and denigration, laughter and tears, it would simply be one parent's account of his daughter's physical growth from milestone to milestone, a notation of dates. To the people who shared and refused to share our joys and pain, anxieties and relief, and to those who continue with us on the extraordinary journey of childrearing, thank you for your humanity, for your frailties and weaknesses, and for your strengths. Bless you all.

To Lynne, for all the joy and love, failure and triumph, pain and understanding, the quarter-century of companionship, and to Becca, for all your innocence and beauty and wide-eyed wonder, I will forever be indebted. Thank you both for allowing me to share your lives.

FOREWORD

Aᴏᴛᴇʀ ᴏᴜʀ ᴇʟᴇᴠᴇɴᴛʜ ᴡᴇᴅᴅɪɴɢ ᴀɴɴɪᴠᴇʀsᴀʀʏ, Lynne and I decided the time had finally come to have a child. We had decided before marriage to establish ourselves fully in our professions before expanding our family because we wanted to provide what we considered was proper care for a child. By age thirty-three, we had become relatively secure in our fields, and the biological clock's constant tick-tick-tick had grown deafening. We were in good physical shape, and our relationship was solid. We were ready for a child — or so we thought.

Impregnation proved no problem. Two months after we ceased contraceptive use, we mounted the camera on the tripod, set the timer, and Lynne poked her stomach out while I, expressing exaggerated wonder and surprise, pretended to listen for fetal sounds through a large plastic cup with the word "Big" scrawled on its side. We sent reprints to dozens of friends and relatives to announce the pregnancy. Lynne was approximately in the ninth week.

A few days after we mailed out the prints, Lynne began to spot blood. Then she passed a large glob of blood-streaked mucus. A subsequent ultrasound revealed she'd suffered a miscarriage, but four months later she was pregnant again. And again, at the same point as the first pregnancy, she began to spot blood and pass mucus.

She sank into a depression on which my antics to cheer had little effect. Perhaps she saw through me, realized that I was dealing internally with my own depression while outwardly exhibiting an it's-for-the-better attitude. Our mothers provided little emotional support, but Lynne finally found comfort in various published accounts of persons who've effectively dealt with miscarriage. While many of the books nobly attempt to address the concerns of both male and female partners who've experienced miscarriage, the advice and comfort falls short for men. The father, in nearly all literature relating to pregnancy and birth, is addressed as secondary parent, the inept partner, despite the everlasting cry for more fatherly involvement in childrearing. I dealt with my own pain through writing. Other fathers deal with it in other ways, but few receive the same kind of comfort so readily and quickly available to mothers experiencing a miscarriage.

Six months following the second miscarriage, we decided to try one last time. Again, impregnation proved no problem. This time, we passed the critical point of nine weeks without incident as Lynne joyously hugged the toilet, vomiting on schedule daily, a good sign that the pregnancy was progressing normally.

Even before the first pregnancy, we had decided that Lynne would continue her career outside the home. Since I was self-employed and worked at home, I would serve as the child's primary care-giver. As the third pregnancy progressed, I searched library and bookstore shelves alike for parenting books strictly for stay-at-home fathers, but what I found were books that addressed only Mom as the spoon-in-the-squished-carrots, wipe-the-butt parent. Dad, on the other hand, was an emotionally calloused idiot who craved sex immediately following the birth, someone who had to be taught to remember occasionally to change a diaper or burp a suckling child. He was an aloof, bumbling, self-centered jerk.

To cope with and explore my nervousness and feelings of inadequacy as a father-to-be, and to attempt to deal with the emotional swings pregnancy causes both parents, I began a journal of notes to our developing child, relating events in our lives, our emotions, and my thoughts on the future and the past. I wanted the child to know who Lynne and I were when we conceived. I wanted the child to see how we grew and developed as it became the central point in our lives. I wanted to communicate directly and immediately instead of recalling years from now through the softening haze of time.

Communication became an obsession then and remains so today. Perhaps it is vanity, but I want to speak to Becca throughout her life, even after my death. I want her to know and remember Lynne and me for more than the parents we have become to her. I want her to know us as people — who we were, who we are now, who we will be. I have written about the pregnancy, about the birth, about Becca's development and accomplishments, about my childhood, about the relationship between Lynne and me, about world events, about my and Lynne's emotional swings, about relatives' reactions to our parenting decisions, about society's faulty assumption that men can't be as nurturing as women —I've written about our lives, together and apart.

I never anticipated or planned for the notes to be published in book form; that came by accident, the result of conversations with other parents expressing a desire to read more personal father-oriented material. To protect the privacy of friends and relatives, I have changed most of the names within, and, yes, I'm using a pseudonym.

I hope you find value within these pages, perhaps drawing comfort from knowing that others have experienced similar joys and tragedies to your own. I continue to write letters to Becca, describing her growth and accomplishments, the events in each of our lives, and the failures and successes Lynne and I experience as parents and partners. After two miscarriages, a difficult third pregnancy, and a rough first year as parents, Lynne and I have grown immeasurably, both spiritually and emotionally, yet we have so much more growth ahead, so many areas we need to improve. And Becca, bless her, forces us to grow and develop even when we don't want to. For that, we owe her more than we can ever repay during our short time with her.

While many parents view their children as possessions to dominate or clay to mold in their image, we realize that Becca is a unique individual who requires nurturing, not domination, a temporary guest for whom we're responsible. We are obligated to foster and guide her development into a responsible and caring adult, able to accept the consequences of her actions, but we have no right to dictate the choices she must make in life. We owe her our support in good and bad times, when we agree, when we disagree — in short, we owe her our uncompromising friendship and love.

I am extremely privileged and lucky. I've been afforded a remarkable opportunity to take part in the lives of the two most wonderfully fascinating people I have ever known, my best friend, Lynne, and our greatest accomplishment, Becca.

PREGNANCY

Chapter One

29 May

Two weeks ago, my friend Andrew asked, "Why have a child?" I couldn't answer him then, and I can't answer him now. Maybe it's the arrogant desire to live beyond the grave, to continue Lynne's and my particular family lines. Maybe it's vanity—"Hey, look. Told you I could procreate!" Or, maybe it's a need to be a good parent, to prove to myself I can succeed where my parents failed. Maybe it's a combination of all.

But what *right* do Lynne and I have to create another life? Because God supposedly instructed Adam and Eve to do it like rabbits? Simply because a person is sexually equipped to get a new life started doesn't qualify him or her for the role of parent. Adoptive couples and singles are scrutinized closely—evaluated and tested for being suitable parents. Maybe it's time to evaluate potential biological parents before they grunt their way into parenthood. If they fail the scrutiny—hey, sorry, no dice. I'm sure that would get people up in arms. But there are too many babies, unwanted and abused, forgotten once they're outside the womb.

You're in the third month of development, resembling a frog more than a human fetus at this point, but I feel I must apologize to you now for the pain and disappointments life will slap you with in the years to come. And I also must rejoice in the knowledge that you will experience such wonder and good, perhaps enough to make the short ride called life worthwhile.

Be assured, kid, nothing—once you leave that warm hot tub you're now floating around in—will come easily. You will always pay a price. You will always be forced to struggle against the odds to attain happiness. But remember this during those struggles: If you need Lynne and me or want us by your side, we will be there to help you clarify your goals, to sort through the possibilities, and to assist you in every way we can as you make the decisions you must make for yourself. We'll rush to your defense when you are right, help you face your responsibilities when you are wrong. As long as you want us, we will be there.

In this fourteenth week of pregnancy, we're excited and nervous. Over the last eighteen months, pregnancy has ended twice in miscarriage, the first in the ninth week, the second in the tenth. So you can understand our concern over you. You've survived much longer than the first two, but nothing guarantees this pregnancy—*you*—will go to term. It's a long time and a lot of change for us all to reach Pearl Harbor Day, your projected birth date. Over the next few weeks, Lynne will undergo amniocentesis which will reveal whether you are developing properly and whether you are likely to experience certain genetic complications.

The primary problem now is hives. A thick rash has developed on Lynne's torso, arms, and legs, plaguing her with incessant itching. We hope a visit to her general practitioner later today will clear it up.

Andrew's question nags. Why have a child? Why have you? Ask us in another year, another twenty, or maybe even fifty if we're still around. Perhaps we'll have an answer then. I'm sure we'll have a million justifications, each and every one valid, but will they prove suitable as reasons?

30 May

Lynne has heat-related hives aggravated by pregnancy, according to the doctor. For relief, she can take oatmeal baths and apply natural topical anti-itching cream, but nothing more because medications could affect your development. As for me, I'm weary of running to the bathroom every few minutes. I'm into my third day of diarrhea (a damn near mystical experience you'll probably suffer within your first few months of life). What the hell is this? I thought diarrhea was supposed to be the expectant mother's problem, not the *father's*. Sympathy squirts, perhaps?

We have yet to break the news to any relatives that Lynne's pregnant again. Experience has taught us to keep our mouths shut until we're certain that all will turn out well. In the first pregnancy, as soon as the little home-testing kit indicated "pregnant," we set up the tripod and camera to snap a shot of me kneeling before Lynne, my ear to a cup pressed to Lynne's abdomen as she had poked her stomach out as far as possible. We printed dozens, sent them out as the pregnancy announcement, and, a week later, Lynne began to spot blood — just when the first congratulatory calls and letters started coming in.

Lynne's gynecologist performed an ultrasound, found no heartbeat, admitted her to outpatient surgery, and Lynne had a miscarriage. The entire procedure took only a few hours. We came home. Lynne, depressed and still groggy from anesthesia, asked me to make the calls to immediate relatives, including Elizabeth, her mother. She asked me to assure Elizabeth that she would personally phone in a couple of days when she was feeling better. Two days later, Lynne phoned her mother as promised.

"I just want you to know," Elizabeth stated, "I'm *very* disappointed in you. *You* should have called me; *you* should have told me."

"Mom," Lynne replied evenly, despite the anger evident in her flushing face. "I had just come home from a miscarriage. I didn't feel well, and I didn't feel like talking to anyone. I thought you'd show a little more understanding, realizing what I'd been through." A moment's silence, then

Elizabeth changed the subject, brushing off the incident as nothing more than the popping of a pimple.

We handled the second miscarriage slightly different, not revealing the pregnancy to anyone until well after the miscarriage. We played it cautiously, took our time, and when we were ready and when Lynne was comfortable with what she'd suffered, we told a few relatives . . . who told a few . . . who told a few.

Elizabeth's reaction surprised and disappointed me. I expected her to provide the kind of parental comfort to Lynne that I could not. Instead, she acted insulted by our sadness. She appeared to view the miscarriages as little more than a mild cold, providing no emotional support at all for Lynne. "The people at my office," Lynne told me a couple of months later, "have shown more concern than my own mother."

Dear child, I promise that we as parents will strive to be more to you than what our parents have been to us. When you face a problem of any kind, I hope you'll be able to come to us for the support you need. You shouldn't even have to ask. I hope we never disappoint you with such cold selfishness when you need our understanding, especially under such emotional and traumatic circumstances as miscarriage.

12 June

We breathed a huge sigh of relief Monday. That was the day Lynne and I drove from Huntsville to the University of Alabama genetics clinic in Birmingham for the amniocentesis. We spent part of the morning viewing an amniocentesis video with other couples—most younger than us.

The amniocentesis (a form of ultrasound) proved an amazing procedure. A nurse dimmed the lights, another jellied Lynne's abdomen and pubis, and the doctor, using an ultrasound image to guide his actions, pressed a long needle through the skin slightly below the navel into the uterus. A moment later, a bright star burst at the top of the scanner's screen as the needle broke through the uterine wall. You moved like an acrobat as he withdrew several vials of amniotic fluid to analyze. I mistakenly had forgotten my camera at home, so tense about the procedure.

Results are still a couple of weeks off, but the doctor, as he used the ultrasound to determine your position and size, glanced up at Lynne and then over at me and grinned. "Development, size, movement—it all looks good, pretty normal." And you, tiny tadpole, you swished and kicked and swam even more. You couldn't stay still.

A couple of years ago when Lynne first tested positive for pregnancy, I began a journal like this one, but, after the miscarriage, I deleted all the files from disk. Did the same for the second pregnancy. Today, as I performed cleanup maintenance on the letters disk, I found that I had missed one file, the following, written shortly before the second miscarriage:

9 April 1990

Last night, I dreamed that Lynne began spotting blood the way she did the first time. We went to the doctor, fearing she had already aborted. He injected her womb with some type of chemical to "stun" the fetus, then laid a small, rectangular, flat piece of glass against her vagina. Something black and flea-sized crawled onto the glass. That, supposedly, was the fetus. It hopped around, apparently fine. The doctor smiled, nodded, slipped the glass inside Lynne to replace the fetus where it belonged.

In the second dream, I stood in an area dominated by tall bluffs equipped with stairs for ease of climbing. I was in love with a twelve-year-old girl, and throughout the dream I kept asking myself did I really know what I was doing. "You're thirty-four years old," I argued with myself. Another person, a woman, then led me down a set of stairs toward lapping water. When I stepped onto a stair near the bottom, near the water's edge, it abruptly became water and I went

*under completely, then came straight back up, rising to
the bottom stair where I found myself dry but shaken.
The water then grew gray and similar to wet concrete
in texture, but still lapped at my feet. "Take care," the
woman said, then she faded away.*

*Who knows what they mean? Probably only
my subconscious working out the anxiety over this
pregnancy since the last pregnancy terminated so
unexpectedly. After three months of mental and physical recuperation, we began poking for life again, and it
seems we've connected. This past weekend, Lynne performed a pregnancy test and it came out positive.*

*I began one of these histories during the last
pregnancy, but it ended abruptly. Perhaps this one will
not.*

It did, however. Coworkers and friends provided
Lynne with much tender care, their concern genuine and
comforting. Her colleagues sent flowers; a couple of friends
sent sympathy cards. Folks would ask how she was doing
and nod their relief as she improved, but no one asked about
my own feelings, apparently unaware that a potential father
experiences the same sense of loss as the expectant mother.
Lynne purchased a book on "surviving" miscarriage, but it
and all the other books we searched through considered
women's feelings exclusively. Men, if addressed at all, were
afterthoughts as if society expects us either not to suffer or
to suffer in silence. But the loss is there, deeply felt, and it
has to be expressed in some manner. Some men work it out
with physical labor. I worked it out in words:

Cabinet

*And words were written
to the future,
now a history lost
in the mathematical equations
of my PC;*

It's nearly 10:30 a.m. In a few minutes, I'll leave for what will be the last local TV appearance connected with promoting my first published book. Now that I've been on the interviewee end of the journalist/subject relationship, I can better understand why people immediately regard me with a skeptical eye when I tell them I'm a journalist. As a writer for magazines, I strive to quote my interviewees accurately, cleaning up grammar occasionally, but never changing content. After two newspaper articles about my book appeared, based on interviews the authors conducted with me, I understand why journalists on the whole are held in such disdain. Not only did both writers misquote me, they even *invented* quotes. Amazing. Good thing no one reads past the first paragraph, right?

You remain the headline story in Lynne's and my life. That little heart of yours is pumping away at breakneck speed. We'd planned to buy a stethoscope to listen to your heart as you develop, but we've discovered stethoscopes are next to useless when it comes to locating fetal heartbeats— too many stomach and bowel noises from Mom.

What a day it is. Partly cloudy and breezy, cool for June. Amazingly nice. Wonder what your initial reactions will be to rain, to sunlight, to wind on your face, to snow.

24 June

If puking is an encouraging sign, Lynne's pregnancy is going wonderfully. Up in the morning, and so is breakfast. She's nauseated most of the time and must now eat numerous small meals, up to seven instead of the standard three a day, to counter the nausea and keep the food down, but even that doesn't work every time.

If not later today, then surely by week's end, we should have more than vomit-ability on which to base the progress of this pregnancy. The results of the amniocentesis are due, and we're eagerly awaiting word.

27 June

Last night, around 9:30 or so, not long before heading to bed, Lynne sat reclining, legs stretched out on the flip-up footrest, reading an Agatha Christie mystery as I watched a television show. She suddenly looked up at me, eyes reddening, filling with tears. I bolted forward, afraid. "What? What's wrong?"

She placed the book flat across her thighs, spread her hands gently over her swollen abdomen, and, in a soft and quivering voice, said, "I just felt a flutter."

I laid my hand on top of hers. I had not anticipated how such a simple, natural occurrence could thrill us to tears.

The amnio results still haven't come in. Anxious times. Monday is Lynne's regular monthly pregnancy checkup. Maybe the results will be in by then.

We still haven't informed any relatives of the pregnancy because we're so uncertain it will go to term. We've danced repeatedly around the question of "When are you going to try again?" But Edward, Lynne's brother, asked her directly during their phone conversation last Sunday, "Are you pregnant?" Lynne rolled her eyes, grunted, "No."

Yes, she lied, but we believe it was justifiable. We want to be as certain as possible that you're viable and developing normally—that you will come screaming into this world in a few months—before we breathe a word to anyone. We've grown superstitious: If we brag about an impending event, it won't happen. If you aren't viable, if you aren't developing as you should, we'd rather not endure the reaction from relatives while dealing with yet another—and final—loss.

2 July

Yes! Yes! Exciting news, wonderful news—yes, yes, yes. Yesterday we went in for Lynne's monthly checkup, and one of the nurses, as an afterthought and in her business-as-usual way, said, "Oh yeah, your amnio results came in this morning. Everything looks normal."

Yessss!

Then the doctor fired up the ultrasound viewer, and we watched entranced as you stretched your legs straight out before you, arms and hands starting above your head to drift down as if you were purposely doing a toe-touching exercise. Each time your fingers touched your toes, you jumped as if surprised or tickled. I cursed myself for not having brought in a videotape, but I didn't know they had a recorder hooked up to the ultrasound. Next time they look at you, you'll become a movie star.

Other news pales compared to the checkup, but your Dad-to-be is now a radio personality. I'm talking about an on-air interview I did yesterday at the local public radio station in connection with my book. Did it at lunchtime on the station's Community Forum program, a live, call-in show. Did I say live? It was as near dead as a live program can get, much to the credit of an unprepared host.

As Lynne listened to the interview in her office, she felt you move a couple of times. Were you excited by the fact I was on radio, or were you embarrassed? If the latter, get used to it, kid. I'll probably embarrass you countless times in the years ahead. And I apologize now for all those times—in case I forget to then.

This morning, I phoned my father and told him that you're on the way, the first relative we've informed. He sounded as pleased as anyone can sound while sitting on the john, talking to his son. Why would *any*one install a phone in the bathroom?

Now comes the *fun* as we travel to Pensacola to visit the other relatives and reveal to all finally that Lynne's pregnant. It'll begin tomorrow night with Lynne's mother and grandmother. Then my mother on Thursday, to be followed with the rest at a July 4th get-together.

Well, Becca or Dylan—whichever you turn out to be—you have provided new reasons for insomnia. Sunday night I couldn't sleep for the worry over amnio results; last night, Monday night, I couldn't sleep because I was so excited over the results. What? You meant the sleepless nights have only begun? Just wait 'til you start dating?

16 July

Back from Pensacola, thankfully so. All relatives were duly excited for us, but that's the normal way to be. Lynne's mother crowed, "I knew it, I knew it," when she saw Lynne; my mother "figured you'd be pregnant." Such psychically aware folks!

You, meanwhile, have decided to become a place kicker—and you can't even *think* yet! Well, that's okay. Football players, so I'm told and so it appears by their antics, don't need much of a brain to play anyway. Think of the money you'll make in the big leagues ("big leagues"—is that football or *base*ball?).

To say you've become an active bugger would be understatement. Although you move throughout the day, you are usually most active during mid-afternoon, Lynne says. The "flutters," gas-like movements that Lynne could feel only faintly, began June 22, but, last week, on July 11, she felt your first solid kick against the palm of her hand. The following night, she poked me awake shortly after midnight, took my hand and pressed it to her abdomen just below the navel. A few seconds later, I felt a kick, then another. I sat up in bed, kept my hand there until you finally stopped moving. I couldn't get back to sleep for more than an hour. Since then, you've become quite a dancer or place kicker or whatever you do in there to pass the time. And even when I'm not touching Lynne's abdomen, it's easy to discern when you're moving around. A satisfied, slightly wondrous smile comes to her lips, and her hand goes gently to her belly.

All your increased activity began during a week when your first cousins, Allen and Leigh, ages six and three respectively, were here visiting, sans parents. All the relatives accused us of inviting them to visit so we could practice for you. But that wasn't the reason at all. Lynne and I visited relatives in Florida in January. When we were there, Carol, Lynne's sister, offhandedly suggested we bring her kids home with us for a week or two. We thought it over and decided it might be fun.

The kids, for the most part, had a good time playing in the various local parks, including the Sertoma park where permanent miniature carnival rides are maintained. What the two did *not* enjoy was the structure we placed on their time—in bed by 8:00 p.m., up at 7:00 a.m. And we exacted consistent and specific penalties for inappropriate behavior. When punishment was required, unlike Elizabeth who paddles them with a long, thick wooden spoon, we used "time-out" effectively. We do not believe in corporal punishment for any offense. When you hit, you've failed. By the end of the week, all they needed was the threat of timeout for them to cease any inappropriate behavior.

Despite the fact they had a good time, we were glad to see their parents, Carol and Jack, arrive late Friday night.

With all our other responsibilities and Lynne's condition, we had grown tired and were ready to see them off. Saturday morning, when the kids realized their parents were here, they immediately reverted to their previous behavior patterns.

Over the weekend, Lynne, Carol, Jack, the kids, and I drove up to Tennessee to tour a flour mill from the 1800s era. The mill is still operative and powered by a dammed stream. Interesting sight, the old building set back into thick woods.

After waving good-bye to them Sunday morning, Lynne and I ordered your crib/bed, which is due in tomorrow. We also sorted through most of the items that Carol and Jack brought up—clothes, a baby swing, some toys, and other miscellaneous baby stuff. Because of your grandmother's and great-grandmother's overkill buying habits, Carol had so much for Allen and Leigh that at least one-third of the clothing has never even been worn.

Speaking of grandmotherly spending habits, that will probably prove a point of confrontation after you're born. On Allen's last birthday, Elizabeth and Ann gave him a party, but invited mostly adults. From his grandmothers alone, he received so many presents that he spent a solid hour (I do not exaggerate) ripping packages open as quickly as he could, tossing the gifts aside to open more. Some relatives and friends were so appalled, they invented excuses to leave. Too much. Far too much.

We won't allow that kind of over-indulgence with you. Rest assured, you will have what you need, probably much more, but we won't allow you to be spoiled. To survive in society, to be a productive member, you must learn the value of giving and receiving. That's something all relatives—not only Elizabeth and Ann—will have to understand. Even if they don't understand, they will have to accept it.

Chapter Two

17 July

Lynne's blistery hives improved somewhat yesterday, the result of taking a couple of Benadryl tablets Monday night. Although several of the splotches persist, especially on her stomach and around the bottom of her bra, she refuses to take any more antihistamine unless the itchy blisters reappear on her legs, back, and arms and grow unbearable. She's afraid that consuming too much medication might harm your development. She'll continue to bathe in oatmeal and spread on other natural topical anti-itch solutions. And she'll continue to scratch and endure.

18 July

Your crib/bed has arrived. With no one from the store to help, I grunted and cursed all those boxes containing the various pieces into the pickup last night and brought them home. Then, heaving like an ape needing steroids, I nearly squashed Lynne between the door and wall with one of those boxes as she held the kitchen door open. Some five boxes contain the separate bed parts and nearly fill your room. Now comes the unpacking and assembly of all parts into what we hope will last you until your teen years at least.

We also bought a video camera yesterday, but the thing apparently has a defect, a short in the connection between camera and power supply. I'll be returning it shortly. Perhaps this weekend, the video production of the pregnancy and your arrival into this side of life will begin, with such amazing footage as "Cravings," "Bedroom Transformations," and interviews with the ecstatically nervous parents-to-be!

In other spending (oh is it hard to let that money go!), we bought two stuffed toys for you this past weekend to accompany the musical train engine from Granny (Ann). We purchased a cow puppet we call Sir Loin and a droopy old dog now known as Ms. Bea Itch.

In an otherwise vacant corner of your room, a small rocking chair awaits your tiny butt. It's even equipped with a music box that plays "Rock-a-Bye Baby" when the chair is rocked continuously. The chair is the same one Lynne rocked in as a toddler thirty-four years ago. Its design is simple, a cut-away wooden pail situated on rocking legs. Through the years, moving and neglect battered and bruised the chair until it was barely hanging together. Two years ago, I disassembled the chair, refinished the parts, and reassembled it. A few weeks ago, we located a mail-order shop that sold music boxes designed for rocking chairs. I preferred a song different from "Rock-A-Bye Baby," but that was the only one their boxes played. It's a really sick song if you think about it. "Down will come baby, cradle and all" (and to the hospital we will rush you, broken bones and all). Lynne will complete the rocker with a custom seat cushion so you won't have to rest your buns on hard wood.

While we are trying not to grow overly confident, we're feeling more comfortable about your eventual arrival, enough to ask some friends to serve as more than friends after the birth. Lynne has known Dana and Paula Barr since her early teens. They have repeatedly earned our trust and respect by the way they reared their two sons, now both grown. They treated them with respect and understanding and provided moral and ethical and spiritual support, even when they disagreed with the decisions their kids made. We believe they would treat you as we would, with respect and

dignity as an equal, not as a possession as some view their children. So we've sent them this letter.

> *18 July*
> *Dear Paula and Dana,*
> *. . . We don't want to offend anyone if there's no need to. Now that we're becoming parents, we're trying to cover as many bases as possible, and one of those bases is preparing for the worst, the possibility that we may die before the child becomes an adult, in which case a guardian must be designated. We are currently composing our wills, and we have decided to designate, with your permission, the two of you as guardians in the event of our deaths. Do not feel obligated to say "yes." We will not be offended in the least if you decline. We realize that we are not asking a simple favor. We're asking you to commit to the possibility of devoting a good portion of your lives to rearing yet another child when most people your age by then would be enjoying retirement. So please think it over carefully, and if you decide you cannot make that commitment, that's fine. We'll just hunt you down and beat you into submission. Not really. Again, do NOT feel obligated. Even if you accept, we will list a couple of other people as alternatives. In the meantime, not a word to anyone—especially Elizabeth, Ann, Carol and Ed—for feelings' sake. Give this request serious, considered thought. A "yes" could commit you to far more than you want. When you've decided, let us know.*
> *Yes, well, time to take that blasted camcorder back for an exchange. Looking forward to seeing you. Maybe you both can visit soon; if not, perhaps, Paula, you can make it up with Elizabeth . . . .*

Paula and Dana became friends with Elizabeth long before I met Lynne. As a teenager, Lynne babysat both of their sons. Over the years, the Barrs have proved good and fair people (though Dana likes to cheat at cards and board games—knowing that everyone is aware, yet denying it completely), people we feel comfortable with in designating as guardians—although we certainly hope the eventuality never occurs.

Lynne's hives have improved even more since last writing, though itching persists, especially at night. The bed may wiggle for a quarter-hour nonstop before she finally slips into sleep, but even then she scratches. Her skin where the hives were most prevalent, mainly where clothes touched constantly, looks as though it is in the final stage of healing from severe burns. The doctor warned her the hives could leave scars. "That's the way it goes," she says, and she smiles, places her hand on her abdomen, and is reassured that her suffering is worth it when she feels you move.

You're becoming increasingly active, kicking and poking, but each time I try to feel your movements, you stop as soon as my skin touches Lynne's. What's this hide-and-seek game, kid? A preview of things to come?

As for me, I'm having a nasty bout with hay fever today. I never had problems with allergies of any kind until the fourth year we lived in Honolulu, Hawaii. Shortly before we moved back to the mainland, I'd developed such allergic reactions to pollen and air pollutants in the Islands that I had to take allergy shots twice monthly.

Weather's cloudy, muggy, and hot, and Lynne's certainly suffering the heat's effects. She arrives home each day physically drained and scratching, the heat only aggravating her itching. She plops on the couch, belly bulging, and rests her feet on the coffee table, dozing if I don't engage her in conversation. Last night, she announced tiredly, "I've begun to bow my back when walking to compensate for the weight of the baby."

"What would happen if you didn't?" says I.

"I'd tip over."

22 July

Tons of Allen's and Leigh's baby clothes are drying on the line right now, far more than I thought were in the boxes Carol and Jack brought up when they visited a few weeks ago. Even more await. Despite the fact that the clothes are for boys and girls, I'm washing all since most can be worn by either sex.

We assembled your crib/bed this past Saturday and hung a print of "Starry Night," a painting by Van Gogh. (Yes, he's the guy who cut off an ear. Maybe that gives you an idea of our artistic taste, a bit off-center either in the work or the artist, usually both.) We captured the entire process on time-lapse video. We call it a "pregumentary," a documentary of the pregnancy, beginning with an obviously pregnant Lynne confirming the pregnancy with a positive test strip, followed by the crib assembly, interviews of each of us, skits that encompass such wonders as cravings, and much more to come. By the time you read this, you'll know all about the video. In fact, you'll probably have seen the video so many times, you'll be sick of it.

For now, though, you're content to kick and poke harder, causing Lynne to giggle occasionally. And even I've caught fleeting sensations against my palm before you realize I'm trying. You stop almost immediately after I place my hand on her abdomen as if you're toying with me.

National Public Radio news this morning reported that the Philippines' population will probably double within the next thirty years, which falls in line with the multiplying of the global population. In our childhoods, three billion people populated this planet. Now the number's around seven billion. By the time you're our current age, it'll be fifteen billion. We have in that way condemned you to a worse world than the one we grew up in. You will face more famines and social disorder than we have, but we can only hope the world will survive and that you will flourish. While we can't guarantee anything beyond immediate care, we will attempt in every way to make your life a better one than the lives we had as children and young adults, but you will have to take the initiative. The struggle will be considerable, but not insurmountable.

We will always be there for you. Always.

23 July

Okay, you bugger. It's time we had this out. Every time I try to feel your kicks, you stop. What's the deal? Even so, I still "sneak" a feel on occasion—like last Sunday. We were driving home after visiting one of Lynne's coworkers where we had a relaxing late lunch. I placed my hand on her stomach and felt the oddest sensation against my palm, as though you were tap dancing against the uterine wall—tiny, regular, padded thumps. I can't describe the wonder and satisfaction I felt, overwhelmed only by the doubts in my ability to be a good parent. Last night, Lynne and I watched in near disbelief as you knotted slowly up on one side, causing her abdomen to grow extremely lopsided. This whole process is so truly magical, and it's frightening, a journey like none I've ever taken.

Another incredibly hot day today, in the upper nineties by eleven this morning. It's nearly one in the afternoon, and I've completed a short story I'll send on its maiden voyage tomorrow. It's a monster story that editors may find predictable, but it won't be the first, probably not the last.

Predictable may be the story, but it sure ain't life. That's why we're writing our wills, as I've already explained to you. It now comes down to putting the words on paper and making everything legal, even though I get the squeamies writing about my mortality. I am not certain what is beyond this life. No credible evidence exists to support any religious claims concerning the afterlife; there is only faith. I've placed faith in too many people, too many religions that have ultimately violated the trust. I want to believe, just as I want to believe aliens from another galaxy regularly visit us. But I cannot believe blindly in any dogma as yet. I need something tangible. What frightens me most about dying is going before you grow up, before I can know you, before I have been able to accomplish certain goals I've set for my life. Egotistical? Yes. And selfish. I so want to know you, to be your friend, to watch you grow through childhood into an adult. And I do want to accomplish my goals—career and social. I do not want to die having spent a useless, meaningless life.

But there are no guarantees; everything ends. Everything. So we prepare for the inevitable in our own individual ways. For Lynne and me, it includes the writing of our wills to ensure your protection and care in the same manner we would protect and care for you ourselves.

24 July

When I began this journal, I simply wanted to maintain a record for you, but it's become much more than that; it has become a means for me to communicate to you over the years. Lynne and I have decided the journal would make an appropriate gift to celebrate your thirteenth birthday, to commemorate your passage into adulthood. In essence, we'll be giving you a written photograph or movie of your birth and childhood, accompanied by a view of us you would not otherwise have.

Lack of sexual activity has a strange effect on a person. Because of the two miscarriages, we decided not to risk a third by continuing sexual relations after verifying we were again pregnant, even though intercourse during pregnancy is considered safe through at least the second trimester. As soon as we discovered that Lynne was pregnant, we reeled in our sex drives.

Sexual drive—both desire and activity—is nothing to be ashamed of, and it certainly isn't *dirty* if part of a healthy relationship. Sex is a natural act between two people who enjoy and cherish each other, an expression of special feelings. But the rules have changed since I was a teenager. Back then, sex wasn't as dangerous as it is today. Sexually transmitted diseases such as Acquired Immune Deficiency Syndrome can kill—slowly, terribly. There's no cure at present, and, despite claims by small-minded morons, it is not a "homosexual disease" or plague from God. Anyone engaging in intercourse with multiple partners or with a promiscuous partner is susceptible. Simply put, getting laid can kill you. Few healthy individuals can survive adolescence without having experienced the joy of sex—the way Lynne and I did, the way we share the joy now. But today you must be far more careful.

No one has the right to demand that you or any other person restrict yourself to one sexual partner or to be completely abstinent. I do have the right, however, to voice an opinion. Between two people who love each other, who cherish each other's company, sexual intercourse becomes more than a physical act. It is an opportunity for more than genital excitement, an opportunity for ultimate intimacy, a wonderful and exciting means to strengthen the partnership lovers form. Choose your partner, or partners, carefully. Go wisely to bed. Demand mutual medical physicals *before* you get involved sexually. Form a close friendship. Respect one another. Love one another. Create a bond that sex enhances. It worked for Lynne and me; it might work for you.

Chapter Three

28 July

A few months ago, my mother and I disagreed over some issue I don't even recall now, but I do recall how that disagreement erupted into argument that ended with her words: "What goes 'round comes around, and I just hope I'm still alive to see it." She was suggesting the relationship you and I develop will be like the one she and I have. Mom and I are constantly at odds, rarely agreeing on any subject, unable to discuss our differences without animosity. But to wish that you and I develop the same lack of understanding and communication is pathetic.

Mom and I communicate on a superficial level. I'm not sure where we failed to develop the relationship most mothers and children have, but we've never been close in a spiritual sense, although, during childhood, I felt closer to her than I felt to my father, primarily because I feared Dad more than Mom. I witnessed countless battles that would begin as shouting matches and then inevitably explode into physical abuse with Dad, once cornered, losing control and striking her. (He never hit me, though. Discipline was left to Mom, and she readily used switches and belts.) Mom and Dad were little more than children themselves, in their early twenties—argumentative and emotional, unable to stay on track, deriding rather than supporting each other.

After Dad and Mom divorced, he grew emotionally, developed and learned. He now conducts himself humanely and without violence in interpersonal relationships. He discusses differences without losing his temper; he understands and respects opposing views, although he rarely changes his own. I no longer fear him. I converse with him as an equal and a friend. I can debate him on a friendly basis without fear of condemnation. But my relationship with Mom is almost the opposite.

Conversations with her rarely end without argument. When she and I are together, the air becomes statically charged as we tiptoe around each other, hoping we each avoid pushing the wrong button with statements taken out of context or misinterpreted. But her argumentative and defensive posture is not limited to me. Holidays and other gathering times have become events that relatives dread. I realize she has grown lonely in the two decades since her divorce, but much of that loneliness can be credited only to her. There's a sad joke among relatives—a bet that's made at each "family" gathering: How long can my mother abide before making a scene? Will she wait through the meal? Or will she choose to pick the fight during the first cup of coffee?

She lives alone and shuns those who care about her. When conflict arises, she appears satisfied, especially when she can assume the role of victim. Before she and my father divorced, she perfected that role, rightfully assumed when so physically abused, but she carried her victim status into all interpersonal relationships. She refused to let the past go.

While Dad and Mom failed miserably in their marriage, becoming involved in extramarital affairs and victims of each other's special kind of abuse (his, physical; hers, mental), she has never accepted any responsibility for the divorce. She has blamed Dad; she has even blamed me. She has become a lonely and bitter woman. And yet that loneliness and its constant display only enhance my guilt for being unable to communicate effectively with her—the way sons and mothers should communicate. We are different people with different ideals and goals, but that shouldn't stop us from being friends. It's a harsh, sad lesson, one I've taken to heart. I must succeed with you. I must become the kind of parent in whom you can confide anything, a parent who will not judge or condemn you for the difficult choices you must make, a parent who will support you even if our values differ (and they will), a parent you can count on. While Mom and I failed, you and I can choose to succeed.

Yesterday, Lynne and I went to *Robin Hood: Prince of Thieves*, a so-so remake of the original "Errol Flynn" *Robin Hood*. Halfway through the film, Lynne moaned slightly, grabbed my hand, and laid it on her tummy. The guy behind us must have thought we were nuts because we were suddenly giggling "wows" and marveling over the acrobatics you were performing. I could feel you roll from side to side, slide up and down, twist and gouge. You're a feisty bugger; your kicks are strong and direct, toes or heel or elbow jabbing repeatedly. This morning as Lynne and I lay in bed watching her belly, you began the dance again—and we saw you kick. It is so bizarre to watch a part of Lynne's abdomen suddenly bulge out as if you were trying to break free. Hang in there, kid. You'll be out sooner than you expect.

I finished constructing your changing table. We couldn't find any ready-made nursery furniture with a moon-and-star theme, so we designed the table ourselves and constructed it from yellow pine. It isn't a bad piece of work, although I made a mistake in the design. The sides incorporate decorative pieces that appear to be convenient handles for moving the table, but they're too fragile for the weight. I've broken one twice already, but each break was clean and quickly mended with wood glue. The sides and back incorporate a crescent moon and star. We'll enhance the room's celestial theme further with photographs we shot of the partial solar eclipse that occurred earlier this month.

We've been working on the "pregumentary." So far, it contains time-lapse construction of your crib and the changing table (which will later serve as either a bookcase or stereo center for you), an interview with Lynne exploring her feelings of pregnancy and your coming birth, and nonsense tidbits such as "Cravings" (a skit where I pig out on ice cream while rifling the refrigerator for pickles).

29 July

Today's visit to the doctor proved quite an experience. Lynne's regular gynecologist wasn't in, and when the substitute walked into the examination room, he began stammering as he spotted the video camera in my hands. "We're making a tape for the kid," I said. "And relatives."

He shrugged and grinned. "No one's done that before," he said, "but sounds good to me." Click, the tape rolled. He grinned at the camera, said, "Hi, folks," then performed the examination with calm authority and explanation as though recalling lines from a well-studied script.

The nurse easily located your heartbeat with the Doptone, an amplified ultrasound stethoscope. Your heart was racing along at one hundred sixty beats a minute, up twenty beats from the last time we were in. A rate of one hundred forty or more, according to an old wives' tale, indicates you are female, but I don't put much stock in old wives' tales; I've known too many old wives. The folks in Birmingham already have your gender as part of their records, but we asked them to keep the information out of the report they delivered to our doctor. As for carrying the camcorder into the examination room, not many patients have gone this far. Most videotape only parts of the actual delivery, not the exams leading up to it, but the doctor and nurses happily cooperated, hamming it up.

Lynne's weight is up more than it should be, now one hundred seventy-two pounds, but, considering the miscarriages, the doctor hasn't complained about it. Besides, the weight will come off after delivery, which, by the way, the doctor recalculated somewhere between November 24 and

November 27. Your development is further along than first thought. You were originally predicted to be a Pearl Harbor Day baby.

A few days ago, I had to take this computer back to the vendor for repair. It's only a few weeks old, yet it has continually failed, so far requiring two new video boards and a new mother board. It appears to be in good working order for the moment now that it's running on a new mother board. Never again will I buy a clone from a local vendor.

Tonight, Lynne and I are meeting a friend, Andrew, at Big Spring Park where a free concert will be held—country and jazz. Now there's a combination.

4 August

Back in the early '70s, I wore peace symbols on my shirt, an American flag sewn to the butt of my jeans, and my hair below my shoulders. Peace and love is what my kind preached; down with war. Every person is basically good, we told ourselves. But I'm older now, and I no longer hold such a naive view of my species. You will learn—by the time you read this, you will have already gotten a bitter taste of the fact—that most people don't give a damn about others, that they're in this life to benefit only themselves and to hell with everyone else.

In the last entry, I had brought this computer home from the local dealer that built it. He had replaced the main circuit board, assuring me that it would run smoothly from then on. Shortly after, the computer began glitching yet again, with each power-up requiring reconfiguration. For a third time, I carried it back, and the technician installed yet another circuit board.

After repeatedly dealing with problems and finding faulty construction within the computer, I went to the dealer, informed him of what I'd found, and said I wanted a refund. I told him that I was tired of inferior work and products. The man cursed me, screaming, "There's nothing wrong with that damn machine. You must have done something to it, and I'm not refunding a dime. If you don't like that, then sue me. But you'd better watch your back." As I was leaving, I met another dissatisfied customer bringing back a piece of faulty equipment.

Jerks like this will plague you throughout life, kid. They'll steal from you, lie to you, cheat you, while pretending to be your best friend. They'll take you for a ride and dump you.

Peace and love? What was I thinking back then?

During all this excitement, you have been rather serene—until today at least. You've done little kicking, but you have gradually bunched up on Lynne's right side numerous times as though you were trying to crawl up into her ribcage. Last night it caused extreme pain and discomfort for her, but she and I believe the discomfort is certainly worth enduring for the result. Today, you've been, as Lynne put it, "Rearranging furniture like Dad." (She gives me a hard time because I am perpetually rearranging furniture in various rooms. She says she doesn't know what to expect when she comes home each day.) Today, you've been kicking, poking, and swimming around. Lynne says you're acting just like me, unable to sit still for long.

It's a hot Sunday, and Lynne's on the couch, reading another "Christie" mystery, listening to Bela Fleck and the Flecktones. I'm back in the extra bedroom, our so-called library and office but more of a junk room, testing out this computer. I hope I've solved most of the problems by properly seating all the boards and connecting all the wires. I've learned an important, though costly lesson by purchasing this computer: Never buy from a one- or two-person operated business unless service on or exchange of the product will never be necessary. Buy instead from large companies where you have some recourse. Fewer locally owned businesses in large cities give a damn whether a customer's satisfied or screwed. Another sucker will come along.

Next weekend, Lynne's mother and grandmother will come for a short visit. They're already asking about the best places to shop. Shopping is their one true hobby. Lynne may go for a short spree, but she won't take part in the typical shopping binge because of her physical condition. Elizabeth usually "power shops," all day, nonstop, breakneck, too much for Lynne at this stage of pregnancy.

6 August

Lynne's working (as a government employee) and probably burning up, unless she's lucky enough to be at her desk instead of doing field work. The temperature outdoors currently stands at one hundred one degrees with a heat index of one hundred ten.

I've been thumbing through a journal I began years ago and kept diligently before we moved to north Alabama in 1986. The journal has regular entries from 1981 through 1986, with a few sporadic entries through 1990. Some of the entries find me blushing as I read them now. How naive those scribbles appear to me now, probably the same way these notes to you will appear in ten, twenty, thirty years if I'm around then to read them. I doubt I'd be writing these notes had I found books about fathers I could relate to. Most of the literature pertaining to pregnancy and birth is geared toward women, understandably so, with nearly all fatherhood material on the lighter, comical side, usually portraying fathers as inept and bumbling, certainly incapable of nurturing a child as well as a woman. But I believe the emotionally inept provider role is one that many men assume simply because family and society—like those books—tell us it's the way we should be. Should we? I don't think so.

Men are as naturally nurturing as women, but society has stereotyped both genders into certain roles that most men and women readily fill without question or resistance. Then we complain about our role—rather, we complain about the other's role, unable or unwilling to figure out *why* each behaves so stereotypically male or female. Lynne and I are different in that respect. In this neighborhood, I'm one of the few men who does laundry, vacuums the carpet, makes the bed, cooks a meal, and on and on. Males don't have to be macho to be *men*. You don't have to be a redneck, nor do you have to be oozing virility. And expectant fathers—at least *this* expectant father—experience the same kind of fears and anxieties as expectant mothers. In some respects, pregnancy and birth may be even more difficult for men because we are powerless to quell the pain the expectant mother must endure. A man cannot provide the physical comfort the woman craves, nor can he soothe her worries over the safety and viability of the developing fetus because he has his own to deal with. Yet, he stands more alone and helpless than the woman, in some cases needing more understanding but nearly always receiving less because he is a man, and society preaches that men cannot experience the same emotional depth as women.

You now spend several hours a day in a hard knot rammed under the right side of Lynne's ribcage, causing her great discomfort and sometimes difficulty in breathing. Last night you became extremely active during the early evening. Lynne saw you move a couple of times, and I felt distinct punches and rolls against my palm.

Relatives in Pensacola—Elizabeth, Ann, Bessie, Jack, and others who believe they can predict the future—have pronounced you will be a boy. Not so, says the woman next door. She maintains emphatically you're a girl. She bases her choice on the heart rate theory. She claims boys' heart rates are never consistently above one hundred forty beats a minute, but yours have never been below, with most above one hundred fifty. Where have we placed our bets?

When we decided to have a child, Lynne and I believed that everything would go perfectly, just like a fairy tale. We'd get pregnant immediately (we did, more or less), the pregnancy would proceed without problem, and she'd give birth to a girl, exactly what we wanted. But fairy tales have a way of becoming nightmares. After two miscarriages, the gender no longer matters. We simply want you to arrive healthy, with a normal brain and a sturdy body.

12 August

The weekend with Elizabeth and Ann is over, but there is still a conflict with them. They wanted to buy, buy, buy for you—not even knowing your sex or what you'll need. Toys, clothes, mementos. Were we surprised? Not really. I've already related their propensity for overkill gift giving. We will ultimately be faced with angry confrontation, I believe, but we must maintain our resolve. If they refuse to respect our wishes in rearing you, or if they insist on lavishing you with gifts inappropriate for the occasion and your age, we will either return the gifts to Ann and Elizabeth or donate them to charity. Elizabeth and her domineering style pose a difficult challenge. She is not one who accepts direction from others, but you are our responsibility, and our responsibility to you is to rear you in the best manner we can. That kind of rearing does not include spoiling you with gifts—not from us, not from your grandparents.

As for my mother, Bessie, overindulgence won't be a problem. She is, for lack of a better word, cheap. With her, it appears the confrontation will arise over visitation during and after the birth. Last weekend, she phoned to say she plans to visit "as soon as you let me know Lynne's gone into the hospital." Elizabeth surprised us on this point. We anticipated reluctance from her, but she expressed understanding of our desire for a private birth and chance to get to know you before relatives crowded in to get a peek. Before she and Ann left, she said, "I'd like to be here for the birth, but I understand, so we'll see you in Pensacola afterward." Perhaps we should take that as a hopeful sign. Perhaps she will understand about gifts as easily.

In reply to my mother, I explained, "We prefer no one to visit during the birth and hospital stay because we want time to adapt as a family. We don't want to be worried about entertaining a houseful of guests. We'll be down to visit everyone in December or January. (Both sides of our relatives live in the Pensacola area, except for my father who lives in south Alabama.) You're welcome to come any time before delivery, but not during and not immediately after." She responded with little more than a grunt.

You are growing rapidly now, your kicks and punches becoming stronger by the day. While your punches occasionally hurt Lynne, your squirming tickles. I envy the special feelings she must be experiencing. I can only imagine them by feeling you with my palm; I can't fathom what it must feel like to carry you *inside*. Lynne is never alone as you constantly squirm and adjust yourself. I sympathize for the discomfort she must endure—backaches, constipation, nausea—but she is experiencing an inexplicable and enviable closeness to you that I will never fully understand or enjoy. She is extremely fortunate.

19 August

Last weekend, you kicked up a storm, as the saying goes. Lynne began to giggle Sunday afternoon, raised her blouse, yanked the waist of her skirt down, and we watched a good fifteen minutes as you kicked, rolled, and poked. In another week or two, your movements should be defined enough to videotape for the pregumentary. In about sixteen years, you'll be grumbling, "Mom, Dad, don't show *that* again" as your boyfriend or girlfriend makes himself or herself comfortable on the couch.

Our lives are going along smoothly at present. No more dealings with the builder of this computer, even if it blows up. And our mothers have apparently accepted and respect the requests we've made concerning you and birth. Lynne called her mother Saturday and explained our feelings on gift buying and giving. She said there were a lot of "Yeses" and "Okays," but she wonders if the message sank in completely. You must learn to value the gift and the act properly; you cannot do that if every whim is fulfilled. I hope you will understand.

26 August

Over the weekend, Lynne made the pad for your changing table. You'll be able to use the pad as you grow older, taking it to preschool for nap time. All that remains in the decorating and furnishing of your room is the cushion for the small rocking chair. Lynne will probably make that this coming weekend, which just happens to be our thirteenth wedding anniversary.

This afternoon will find us in the doctor's office where we hope to hear your heartbeat yet again. I wonder what the rate will be this time.

Chapter Four

4 September

Four productive workdays ended with a break for our anniversary last Monday. We spent a quiet day at home, taking care of odds and ends that included Lynne making the cushion for the small rocking chair.

You proved extremely active again over the weekend, presenting the best exterior view of movement to date. You poked and rolled and squirmed against Lynne's abdomen—wonderfully amazing! An attempt to videotape that kind of movement will come soon and certainly will be incorporated into the pregumentary. We're shooting other scenes every few days now, and I'm sure the finished product will, since it will contain footage of your first year, embarrass you (because the video will catch you unguarded) *and* us (because we will appear so naive and ill-equipped as parents).

Two weeks ago, you'll recall from earlier entries, I was disappointed that Mom didn't understand our need to have a private birth and time alone with you. I was thankful, though, that only one mother chose to question our decision, that Lynne's mother had understood and accepted our wishes gracefully. Then, this past Sunday we received a phone call from Elizabeth. "I'm coming up as soon as you go into the hospital," she tells Lynne.

"Mom, you already . . . ."

"No, it doesn't matter," Elizabeth snaps. "I *should* be there for *my* grandchild's birth."

The sudden flip-flop caught Lynne completely unguarded. Her hands trembled. She said she had to go and hung up. And she began to cry. She explained between soft sobs that Elizabeth had changed her mind and now insisted on being present for everything. As I held Lynne to comfort her, I grew increasingly infuriated. To be so callous to your own daughter involving such a miraculous event—I simply could not and cannot understand.

I realize that our request could be considered selfish, but we feel it is the best course for us. The added stress of having domineering relatives present as we attempt to adapt to such a sudden change in lifestyle would be disruptive and complicated. Elizabeth should be more understanding, if for no other reason, because she's Lynne's mother. But then, she should have been more understanding and consoling after the first miscarriage.

After Lynne calmed down, she and I agreed that talking to her mother again wouldn't work and that we would have to state our intentions in writing. I composed a letter to Elizabeth, friendly but firm, again expressing our need for time alone. Lynne read it and made a few minor changes. The final version reiterated our desire for a private birth in case the delivery proves difficult. And we reminded her that she had agreed to our requests when she last visited.

Lynne and I aren't fools. We realized the risk of pissing off Elizabeth, but we thought she could deal with the situation on an adult level. As an afterthought in the letter, we defined our views on gift giving in an attempt to avoid a more explosive confrontation later on. We stated views that are obvious for anyone who knows us. We are inviting everyone, especially your grandparents, to present you with gifts, but the type and number of gifts must be reasonable and appropriate for the time of year and your age. We will not allow circuses that Leigh and Allen experience. Those children have been so buried under the guise of benevolence that the value of giving and receiving has become a mystery to them. We will not allow that to happen to you.

10 September

We attended the first of the birthing classes last night and viewed a film that provided a quick and glossy overview of what expectant parents should anticipate during the various trimesters—a bit late for the first two trimesters since this class doesn't even begin until couples are at least midway through the third. After the film, the instructor, a former delivery-room nurse, directed the women to sprawl on the floor on their assorted blankets and pillows to begin learning such mystical childbirth techniques as proper delivery room breathing. Puff, puff, damn the husband. She then demonstrated certain exercises the women could use to strengthen back and pelvic muscles used for delivery. The exercises amount to little more than isometrics of the spine, pressing the small of the back to the floor in a modified sit-up. Upcoming classes will consist of more exercises and coaching, and the instructor said she'll delve into greater detail about the birth itself—"how to keep the husband from passing out," she laughed.

Get wise, lady. It's the '90s. We men aren't all chauvinistic putzes incapable of empathy or sympathy pains. Hell, we even wash dishes and wipe babies' butts, despite the fact that we don't have the same conveniences afforded moms, such as changing tables in department stores. (I wonder if society's perception of men's roles will have changed much by the time you grow up and have your own children. One gauge would be the availability of changing tables in men's restrooms. Few public places—clothing shops, restaurants, grocery stores—provide men with convenient changing-table locations. Mostly, changing tables are in women's restrooms. What does this mean to you and me? When you need a diaper changed in a place that doesn't provide a changing table, I'm going to bare your butt to the world in the most conspicuous spot in the store, especially if it's a really messy diaper. Think they'll get the message?)

Remember the letter to Elizabeth? As I explained, Lynne and I composed the letter after Lynne's telephone conversation with her mother.

> *Dear Elizabeth,*
>
> *Time's getting closer. Yesterday, we watched the kid moving Lynne's innards around. Pretty amazing stuff, and we didn't even have to pay seven bucks a piece to get in for the show . . . .*
>
> *. . . Lynne just got off the phone with you, and she said you're planning to come up after the baby's born. She's upset and so am I. We have already expressed our wishes to everyone in all families and we require those wishes to be honored by everyone. To put it bluntly: We don't want ANY visitors after the birth until specifically invited—and that includes all mothers and fathers and aunts and uncles and grandparents and cousins and friends and enemies and anyone else. Depending on when the baby is born, we will be down in December or January. That is when you and everyone else will meet the child.*
>
> *To explain our reasons again: We will use those first few days and weeks after the birth to get to know one another, to become a single family unit. We will accept no intrusion on that time.*
>
> *Since I'm putting my pen-foot down, while you were up last time, the topic of giving to the child at Christmas and birthdays came up. Lynne and I have talked it over now. We believe that if a child receives a deluge of gifts and toys, he/she will have at best a difficult time learning the value of giving and receiving and the value of things. In short, many gifts breed many problems. If you feel you must over-indulge, then do it by opening a bank account for the child's education and future, not by spending the money on "batteries not included . . . ."*

> *. . . You, and anyone else, however, are wel-*
> *come through October (by November, Lynne will not be*
> *"up" enough for entertaining). Maybe you can make it*
> *before then. Otherwise, we will see you in Pensacola*
> *after the birth.*
>
> *Tomorrow marks our thirteenth wedding*
> *anniversary. What're we doing to commemorate?*
> *Watching Lynne's belly grow, of course.*
>
> *Take care,*

Too harsh? Too *cruel*? Lynne has attempted to phone her several times, but Elizabeth has not returned the calls. And she's probably lumped me into the same category as Ed's wife and Carol's husband, those mooching, lousy in-laws.

Lynne will attempt another phone conversation with Elizabeth in a week or so—not to surrender to Elizabeth's whims, but to reaffirm our wishes and intentions and ask for cooperation and parental support instead of antagonism. I may not be able to answer Andrew's question as to why we're having you, but I know it does not involve pleasing your grandparents.

17 September

The saga develops. Carol and Ed have talked with Lynne since last writing, revealing that Elizabeth has pro-claimed to relatives one and all that we sent her a "scorch-ing" and "scathing" letter in which we state she can *never* see *her* grandchild.

What? What? Did I miss something?

We anticipated an angry response, but not one so absurd and childish and based on lies. I suppose we should have, however, looking back over the years. Elizabeth has a long history of feuds. In fact, in the relatively short while I've known her, Elizabeth has not been speaking to some relative at any given time. While Lynne is tough, I know Elizabeth has hurt her deeply, and I'm afraid the increased stress over her mother's insensitivity could have dire effects on the pregnancy and your development.

25 September

Another visit to the doctor Monday and another A-Okay checkup. Your heart beat at a strong one hundred fifty-four thumps a minute. I asked the nurse about the proposition that high heart rates indicate a female fetus; she laughed. "It sometimes seems that way," she said, "but it could simply be a boy with a fast rate. My son's was fast every time."

Mom, who at first declared you a boy, has now changed her mind. "It's a girl," she says.

"How do you know?" Lynne asked her over the phone.

"I can tell by the sound of your voice."

It appears that our relationship with our mothers has begun to dominate these notes, but those women and their actions occasionally overshadow and mute otherwise joyous events. While they can never diminish our excitement and delight over Lynne's pregnancy, they do prove distracting. Tonight Lynne will again attempt phone contact with Elizabeth to discuss Elizabeth's anger and the tales she's spreading to other relatives about the "scathing" letter we sent.

Lynne's understandably anxious about calling, but she plans no angry confrontation, only an adult examination of the problem. I'm certain Elizabeth will continue to portray herself as victim in this feud, as she has in most others, but that doesn't worry me. I'm concerned only that her actions may have an adverse effect on Lynne by increasing harmful stress. I've said it before: A mother should have more concern and respect for her daughter. Has she forgotten her own pregnancies?

I hope we will not become your enemies, but instead I hope that we can earn your friendship and trust as two people you can count on during bad and good times. What's the use of families whose members do not support one another or who bicker so bitterly over the slightest disagreement?

Lynne has definitely entered the physically draining phase of pregnancy. She is exhausted by the end of each work day, but, despite her fatigue, she continues to walk after work as often as possible to exercise herself and you. And you, kid, you're something else, a regular athlete. Your rolls and twists and pokes enthrall me as I sit for occasional half-hour stretches, watching you go through your acrobatics.

We've been buying *stuff* for you again. Last week, we purchased another book, *Curious George*, one of Lynne's favorites, and this week we'll add another title to your Dr. Seuss collection. And then there's *The Giving Tree*, a wonderful book of ultimate charity and ultimate greed.

It's 2:30 in the afternoon, and I've finished a first draft chapter for a book I began shortly after I started these notes to you. I'm tired, eyes are burning, mind's sapped, but I have a bit more to do—specifically, enter the first drafts of several poems into the computer. Three of those poems concern the pregnancy and you; another concerns Elizabeth's reaction. I'll enter them into these notes later. One is entitled "Lump," the name we've given you for now because you have a talent for lumping into a knot on Lynne's right side as though you're looking for a way out. Be cool, kid. You'll be out soon enough. Then you'll want right back in.

28 September

Back flips, lumping, juggling innards—you're doing it all. Last night, we tried to capture your movements on videotape, but we weren't successful because your activity proved too subtle. From now on, I'm keeping the camcorder within easy reach in case you start your more enthusiastic abdominal acrobatics.

Lynne phoned Elizabeth last Wednesday, but Ann, Elizabeth's mother (Elizabeth lives in her mother's house), told Lynne, "She's at work." Lynne rolled her eyes. Elizabeth is not one who works overtime. "She won't be in until late tonight." Lynne called again Saturday morning shortly after 8:00, but Ann told her, "Elizabeth's gone into town to buy tickets for the Judds concert." Lynne gave another roll of the eyes.

"Have her call me when she comes in," Lynne said to her grandmother.

"I'll tell her, Lynne," Ann replied, "but I don't think she will." Her words were clipped, sullen.

"Why not?" Lynne said. She already knows.

"Y'all hurt Elizabeth more than you know," Ann said, and she began to cry. "To tell her she can't see the baby . . . ."

"We never said she couldn't see the baby," Lynne fired back, her voice shaking, eyes reddening. "All we did was ask for some privacy—and she already agreed to that."

"You hurt her terribly."

Lynne refused to cry until she hung up the phone. The tears weren't so much over the pain her mother is attempting to inflict, but over the fact that other relatives believe her mother, without question, that Lynne and I would purposely hurt Elizabeth or any relative. Lynne's a strong woman. You would have been as proud of her as I am. She maintained excellent control over her voice as she told Ann, "It's fine if Mom doesn't want to talk to me, but nothing came as a surprise to her. She knew what we wanted. We explained everything to you and to her the last time you were visiting. We explained how we need time to become a family before we have visitors. Y'all agreed, and I am not changing my mind, no matter how childish she behaves. I'll be here if she wants to talk to me, but I will not be calling her anymore. This is not her pregnancy, not her baby. It's *mine. My* feelings and *my* needs are what's important in this, not hers."

Lynne will eventually reconcile with Elizabeth, if allowed, and she might even forgive her in time—but I won't forgive Elizabeth because of what she's done to Lynne and for the grief and unwarranted stress. I can see disappointment in Lynne's eyes, and I can see a certain sadness when we discuss her mother. She wanted her relatives, especially Elizabeth, to rejoice in her happiness over you, but the one relative who should be most understanding and conciliatory is exhibiting inexplicable and unforgivable cruelty.

I suppose she is a good person at heart, only her heart is governed by infantile emotions. Her behavior is beyond reason. If she was concerned and placed her children's well-being before her own, as we're naively taught mothers always do, she would not go to such bizarre extremes to hurt Lynne and endanger you.

We attend the fourth birthing class tonight. Scheduled are a couple of films on delivery, the blessed event that our instructor laughingly claims we pathetic, weak husbands may not be able to handle. Next week we'll tour the hospital's delivery room. Then, for the sixth and final class, the nurse will cover general infant care. That's an area I believe should have been explored for at least four classes. When I think of the responsibility ahead, my stomach begins to flip. No matter how well a parent-to-be prepares, he or she remains pathetically inept.

Chapter Five

8 October

You were ticking away at one hundred forty beats a minute yesterday, or so the nurse estimated from the eight to ten seconds she could focus on your heart. This new nurse was a lot like my father's youngest sister, a mint-julep woman sashaying to her own inner drawl. At first, she could locate only gurgles in Lynne's stomach, but when she finally zeroed in on your heart, it was only momentary, not long enough for a good count, a fact you'll be able to hear for yourself when you're older. What? I haven't mentioned it already? I've been recording on audio cassette your heartbeats and the doctor's comments each time we go in for a checkup.

If Lynne grows much bigger and complains much louder, I may have to buy a wheelbarrow to haul her around so she won't have to walk. You've grown to the point that breathing for her has become a chore. Even when she's relaxing on the couch or lying in bed on her side with the pillows tucked between her knees and against her back as the books instruct, she groans from the discomfort. And constant indigestion nags relentlessly, keeping her awake late each night. She's taken to sleeping, if you can call it that, on the couch in a slightly reclined position, propped up on two pillows, feet supported by the recliner's footrest.

And me? According to all the womanly advice and wisdom floating around, I should be having the time of my life, drifting along as usual (which means scratching my crotch, drinking my beer, and belching between rants at the football referees on the TV screen), pointing at Lynne, bragging, "Yeah, yeah, I did that," all the while expecting her to perform at some prepregnancy mythical level, preparing my meals, washing my clothes, and doing her duty (at least part of it) in bed. But no one's ever called me *normal.*

In fact, I am *not* sleeping well either. If she groans, I'm sitting up, asking, "You okay? You need something?" After all, you're in the last trimester and premature deliveries are not uncommon in difficult and high-risk pregnancies. Perhaps I'm experiencing sympathy pains and discomfort. More likely, it's the stress keeping me awake, the worry about Lynne and you, her mother's reaction, who might misunderstand next, what could happen if . . . . I routinely drop off around 11:00 p.m. to wake by 4:00 a.m. when, unable to go back to sleep, I rise, do a few situps, pushups, stretches, then head for the park for the daily five-mile jog. The body's tired each night by bedtime, but the brain keeps on ticking, unable to switch off.

Mom has decided to visit this weekend since I told her, as she puts it, "to stay away" during the birth and days following. Virginia, my cousin who's like a close sister, will come with her. My mother has visited us only one other time since we moved to Huntsville (she never visited us in Hawaii). Five years ago, she chose the day we moved from an apartment into this house to drop in. Virginia came then as well because Mom will not travel the three hundred miles alone. I believe she brings Virginia to act as a barrier or referee between us, to prevent or discourage arguments, or perhaps to avoid direct conversation at all.

As your delivery draws closer, Elizabeth continues to refuse direct communication with us. If she truly feels slighted or hurt by our requests and our needs, she should confront us directly, explaining her feelings while attempting to understand ours, instead of spreading the lie that we've for-

bidden her from ever seeing you. If nothing else, our mothers are educating us about the kind of parenting we must always avoid.

Ed and Katrina will also be stopping by this weekend, on Sunday as they head for Nashville on a short vacation. And in a week or so, Carol and Jack and Paula and Dana may come in for a firsthand gape at the ever-expanding Lynne. Anyone else with the inclination to stop by, including Elizabeth and Ann, is certainly welcome until the end of October when delivery time will be too close for us to worry about entertaining guests.

14 October

Mom did a no-show last weekend. She blamed her car—some unspecified repair needed—but, as far as Virginia knew, Mom had simply changed her mind. She now plans to visit over the weekend of October 21. That's the last weekend we'll willingly accept visitors, I told her. We wouldn't want a surprise from you while we had a houseful of relatives.

Ed and Katrina stopped by Saturday afternoon on their way to Nashville for their "last vacation before having children." I could be wrong, but, between you and me, kid, I don't believe they're ready for parenthood. I don't believe *anyone* is ready for parenthood, especially those two. They've been married two years now, and their tolerance for one another is so limited they can't be together for more than a few minutes before sailing willingly and vocally into an argument over the slightest of disagreements. If their tolerance for one another is so limited at this point, how can they expect to cope with the demands of a newborn *and* a marital relationship?

We ate dinner at a favorite pizza parlor, and Katrina bought you two receiving blankets and a bed blanket because, according to her, Elizabeth has nixed all attempts by relatives and mutual friends to give Lynne a baby shower. "She said she didn't want anyone to because y'all told her she could never see the baby," Katrina said. Oh, it is so tempting to do exactly that, but we aren't that cruel. We simply require initial privacy. That's all. We want you to meet your relatives, especially those like Elizabeth and Mom, just to experience their bizarre natures firsthand. You can't take our word for it. You'd never believe us.

Birth preparation classes ended last night with a couple of films on feeding and infant care, the extent of training for taking baby home. Hey, folks, I could use just a tad more advice and instruction in this area. Even though I'm eager for your arrival, kid, I am exceptionally anxious and feeling far underqualified to handle the job ahead. I don't want to screw up in your rearing, and I'm afraid I might. A person tends to repeat the mistakes of his or her parents, but I want so much for you to experience the good things of life without the parental antagonism that Lynne and I endured throughout our childhoods. We want you to develop into the best person you can be. As one narrator of the PBS series "Childhood" put it, children are their parents' messages to the future. I want our message to be one of wonder and joy and beauty and light. But are we capable of providing you with the nurturing environment you need to develop into a confident and compassionate human being? We have only one chance, but what if we blow it?

Lynne took today off from work to complete her Christmas shopping for me, not that it matters much to me whether I receive a gift on Christmas Day. As for my shopping for Lynne, I want to buy a few more stocking stuffers, but, for the most part, it's done. Christmas giving to one another this year isn't going to be as extravagant as the last couple of years simply because you're coming. Our minds and money have been preoccupied with getting the house ready for your arrival.

Meanwhile, you're still playing your move-and-hide games with me. You'll twist or turn or kick, and Lynne will

nudge me or gasp, "Look!" But when I turn, her abdomen's taut and smooth, glassy as a calm lake. Is this indicative of things to come? Must I place locks on the closets as soon as you learn to crawl?

18 October

Lynne's been riding an emotional roller-coaster since pregnancy began, blaming it on varying hormone levels. But maybe *my* hormones are acting up as well. In the last few weeks, I've grown edgy, quick to the fight if challenged over even the mundane or meaningless. On the flip side, I hear on the radio stories of incomprehensible acts and break down. Yesterday, a psychotic person in Killeen, Texas, drove his truck through a cafeteria window at lunchtime, then gunned down some twenty-two people for no apparent reason. I broke into tears. Has lack of sleep finally worn down my mental and emotional faculties?

"You're bringing me into *what* kind of world?" you ask. Crazy, dear child. Insane.

Mom has again asserted her intention to be present for the birth and homecoming, so we've written another letter that may also become infamous in the annals of familial correspondence. We tried a different approach with this one, thanking her for understanding and complying with our wishes. We wrote in first person because that will work better with Mom.

> *Hi,*
>
> *Sorry you couldn't make it up this past this weekend, but you'll have another chance the weekend of the 26th and 27th. If you can't come then, don't worry; we won't be offended, but that's the last weekend we'll be up to entertaining visitors. Lynne will be too tired, and I have much work to complete before the baby's arrival. In the meantime, if you're still trying to decide on some gift as you said you were last week, we could always use some hooded bath towels, as well as crib*

bedding such as a mattress cover or blankets (we have plenty of sheets) . . . .

. . . The pregnancy is going fine. The kid's moving a lot, kicking and gouging. And sometimes it feels like it's picking at Lynne's innards, like a guitarist plucking strings. Lynne has become extremely uncomfortable and has constant indigestion. She can't even get comfortable enough to sleep in bed, so she sleeps on the couch in a half-sitting position.

After the birth, we'll visit Pensacola to introduce the kid to everyone. We'll stay maybe three days or so. I'll let you know exactly when we're coming, which depends on the kid's health and Lynne's recovery time. I certainly appreciate your understanding in our desire to have a private birth and privacy in the days following. We need that time alone to get used to a new person in the family. We wouldn't have the quiet time we need if we had to worry about who's coming and what we have to do to make sure they're comfortable. Not everyone has understood our needs in this area, but I'm glad you do. And don't worry, you won't miss out on anything. I'll be taking pictures galore and there'll be a few other surprises as well.

We've had fun getting the kid's room ready. It's decorated in a sky theme with a print of Van Gogh's "Starry Night" and a picture I took of the partial solar eclipse in July. Why all the sky images? The changing table we built has a crescent moon and star cut into the sides and back. Other decorations will include toys and memorabilia from Lynne's childhood and from mine, if I can locate some.

I need to go. I have work to do.

Take care,

Will it work? We'll know in four to eight weeks.

Think of that. Four to eight weeks and you'll be on this side of the world, an air breather, shedding your gills for jeans and t-shirts. Finishing touches are being done now. What can you see in there? Colors? Can you hear my voice when I draw close to Lynne's abdomen to talk to you? Can you hear the muffled sound of my guitar at night?

It's a beautiful, sunny, warm Friday afternoon. Paula and Dana are due here any time. Paula is so excited about the pregnancy—excited in a maternal way, as though Lynne were her own daughter—and she wants to share as much as possible in our joy while respecting our wishes concerning you.

It's been a hectic week. I haven't accomplished much creative writing, but Lynne and I have completed numerous other chores—among them, the cleaning of a baby carriage, high chair, walker and assorted toys that a friend gave us (his daughter is now five years old); the addressing of baby announcement/Christmas cards; filing all cassettes of interviews concerning family histories; videotaping the guitar instrumental "Dancing Naked" I wrote specifically for the pregumentary; updating the edited master video; and applying for several writing grants I don't have chance in hell of landing.

Earlier today, I purchased this year's proof set of coins and a silver dollar to commemorate your birth. Lynne and I plan to buy a proof set each year from now on to add to your collection.

Next week, Lynne goes in for another checkup, then each week thereafter until delivery. Our "things to do" list in preparation for your arrival should taper off beginning next week. Your room is ready, the announcements addressed with only your name and statistics to fill in after your arrival, the video up-to-date, and the VCR in good working order for all those late-night feedings. In the slack time, I want to get back to my novel. I have only five or so chapters to complete the first draft, and I want to do that before you're born.

Next Friday, I'll be at Lynne's office where her coworkers are throwing a baby shower. I'll shoot video for the pregumentary, of course. The organizing secretary said Lynne's coworkers had collected enough money to buy two nice gifts, including a car seat. In November, which could be your birth month, Lynne is due for promotion to GS-12 just in the nick of time. Another mouth to feed, and a little more money to do it with.

21 October

The Barrs arrived Friday afternoon before Lynne came in from work. Paula was so eager to see Lynne, she was constantly up and down from the sofa to look out the window, hoping to spot Lynne driving up. Conversation before Lynne arrived turned immediately to Elizabeth and the infamous letter we sent. Paula and Dana have known Elizabeth for more than twenty years, but they have never before seen this side of her.

Elizabeth, they said, had mentioned the letter numerous times, claiming that it forbids her to visit us ever, that we insisted she could never see you, but she has not offered Dana and Paula a look at the letter. So I did. When they read the letter, their response to Elizabeth's position was one word: "Stupid." But they know Elizabeth well enough to realize she will not back down from a position she has so vehemently taken. They suggested that Lynne and I write another letter, an attempt to reconcile. We've been considering doing just that since the phone calls have failed, but I wonder what good it would accomplish.

Paula and Dana's visit has reassured me that Lynne and I made the right choice in selecting them to act as guardians in the event of our deaths. They're good people, and they have proved, at least to us, to be able parents, respecting their sons as individuals, not as miniature slaves who must obey and serve. It's refreshing to see that quality in parents. It's a quality we will strive to develop and maintain in our relationship with you.

Mom now plans to visit this coming weekend. She did not mention the letter we sent to her concerning our privacy. I wonder what came between her and me, what specific incident set us on paths that would eventually grow so far apart. She does not approve of my lifestyle, my marriage, my career. Will I be the same with you? Why have children if for only creating new enemies? Never make your choices in life to please Lynne and me, kid. You must choose what's best for you. We can't live your life, and we can't live our lives through you. Make the choices you must make, those that best serve your needs. If we can't understand and support you in those choices, it will be our loss.

It's partly cloudy today, but no rain in the forecast. Tomorrow, another appointment with the doctor, another listen to the heartbeat. Your movements, especially the movements you make low in the uterus, no longer tickle or make Lynne giggle. They have become painful to the point of drawing tears. You continue to grow, and so does Lynne, but, despite the discomfort, she still finds pleasure and satisfaction in the process. Her swelling feet and I have finally convinced her to leave work the week before Thanksgiving (which falls on November 28 this year) instead of working up to the day she delivers as she originally planned. She hopes you'll decide to get on with this side of life beginning Thanksgiving weekend. What a glorious Turkey Day it will be if you decide to pop your head out and say hi.

23 October

With "probably its butt," according to the nurse, riding up in the usual place directly under Lynne's navel, you have now blown one old wives' tale out of the water. Your heart rate yesterday was one hundred thirty-five beats a minute, well under all those previous, and certainly not high enough for the woman next door to continue to predict your gender as female.

We consider sending another letter to Elizabeth, attempting reconciliation while again explaining our position and needs. As I've already said, I don't believe a letter is worthwhile, since Elizabeth will view it as acquiescence and as an invitation to impose herself on us. When Lynne decides to act in matters like this, to write a letter or make a call, I usually prod her along to get it done. "It's best," I say. However, I won't prod this time.

It's overcast and rainy today, just right for sleeping, but Lynne's at work and so am I (as soon as I'm finished with this entry). Another first draft chapter on this dark fantasy novel should be completed by the end of the day. In a week or so, all chapters should be on disk, ready for the first set of revisions.

Last night I dreamed that you were a rather *large* boy—twelve pounds and twenty-three inches long. And I dreamed that my grandfather—"Big Daddy" died two years ago—stopped by at the hospital to take a look at his great-grandson. Your overly large size amazed him just as it amazed the nurses and other parents at the viewing window. He congratulated us, patting our shoulders, shaking our hands, telling us as he did each time we saw him in life that Lynne and I must always love one another, even beyond the grave, that marriage is sacred. Then he said he had to go, and he rushed away, back to wherever he had journeyed from. I watched without ever saying a word, knowing that he was hurrying back to the land of the dead, yet the visit itself seemed natural, a part of life, an everyday occurrence.

25 October

So, what did you think? About my mother, that is. "Old lady Bessie," as she calls herself, is quite an experience, huh? Or could you hear much in that soft, warm oven known as Lynne's uterus? Mom and Virginia arrived a little before 1:00 a.m. Saturday. After a few hours of sleep, I took Mom shopping to places she said she wanted to go, but once we arrived at those stores, she decided she didn't want to look or buy; she was ready to leave. Then she wanted to walk in a forest, so I took her to Green Mountain, a mountaintop lake and surrounding trail (about one and a half miles). Before reaching the halfway mark, she began complaining that the trail was too long, that the day was too hot, that I should have known of a better place to take her. I volleyed jokes with Virginia, avoiding the bait to argue. They left early the following day, and Lynne and I breathed much easier, relieved that they were gone, relieved that it was the last weekend we'd have to worry about guests.

As for the letter of reconciliation, Lynne has decided against it; instead, she wants to confront "Mommy Dearest" face to face. So, kid, your first trip to Pensacola should initiate you well into the interpersonal relations with your relatives. Dealing with them has become anything but congenial. Why? Perhaps we've all become so different, we can't stand one another. Or maybe Lynne and I have finally grown up, have finally asserted our goals and objectives, refusing to be led or dominated by the wishes of any relatives.

You racked up at Lynne's office shower last Friday, kid. They gave you all kinds of goodies—blankets, diapers, toys, and a wonderful safety car seat that should last you through age five.

Received a letter from Paula and Dana a couple of days ago. They have a bet between them on your gender. Paula says you'll be a girl—eight pounds, two ounces; Dana says a boy, eight pounds six ounces. What do you say?

30 October

You're in the home stretch. Pretty much baked and ready to come out of the oven, and it appears you're getting antsy about your pending debut. You're wiggling around, rolling and bunching in corners of Lynne's innards that she didn't know existed—and you don't stop moving even when I look now.

This past Monday morning around 3:30, Leon, one of our cats, vomited on the back of the couch, which, of course, awakened Lynne a few feet away. Instead of waking me to clean up the mess, she did it herself. She cleaned the soiled rag by rinsing it in the kitchen sink. Barefoot and damp handed, she reached for the range-hood light switch, pressed it, and got a slight shock that startled more than hurt. She left the light blazing, returned to the couch, and stretched her palms and fingers lightly over her abdomen, barely breathing, praying you'd move. She waited. She began to cry softly. Then she felt you kick, and a set of knuckles or a knee rolled beneath the skin. More tears, but now from relief. She had been so frightened that the shock had harmed you.

Let's bow our heads in a moment of silence for a passing. Last Sunday, the washing machine, after two years of semi-faithful service, filled its tub and spun its last cycle. I had put in a load of clothes, left them, and returned when the load should have been finished only to find the garage flooded, the machine whining its high-pitched death song. Better now than later, after you arrival when money will definitely get tighter, but we hadn't budgeted for the extra $360 expense this month.

It's 9:00 a.m. Nearly finished with the first draft of the novel. After long consideration and little action on the other end, I've decided to drop the agent representing my work. He isn't hungry enough to market it as it should be. I, on the other hand, *am* hungry, and I've had better results getting my stuff read and published than he has.

Lynne's doing well in her work—for a pregnant woman whose physical movement grows increasingly restricted with each day. "I don't care if it's a boy or girl," she said last night with a heavy sigh. "I'll be glad when it gets here. I just hope it's healthy." I too am ready to move on. Pregnancy has been a wonderful and magical experience, but it's time to move on. I'm eager to get to know you. Whatever you are, whenever you come, we do so hope you're healthy and that life will treat you with kindness.

6 November

Every father and mother I've talked to claims they were able to discern exactly what part of the kid rolled across the abdominal wall in late pregnancy—knuckles, heel, elbow, whatever. Maybe so, but your movements are so varied, active and quick, we can't tell what part of you is moving; head or butt, we don't know. I've leaned in close and asked you to move more slowly a couple of times, but you don't listen. Practicing for the terrible twos already, hey?

On Monday during the weekly visit to the doctor, your heart rate was at one hundred forty-six. Lynne informed the nurse of the swelling in her feet, and when her doctor came in, he said, "So, you're having some swelling."

"Yes," Lynne replied.

"Staying off your feet?"

"No," she said.

"You are now."

Seems the nurse had charted that Lynne was experiencing swelling not only in her feet, but also in her hands and face, a sign of impending fetal and delivery problems. However, the swelling has occurred *only* in her feet. The doctor nodded and mumbled, "Never mind."

Lynne's time at work is groaningly drawing to an end. Two weeks, two days to go. And I have completed the first draft of the novel I've been working on for what seems like forever. I should finish a final draft to begin the submission process sometime during the first half of next year—depending on you and my abilities to care for you. Have I mentioned this before? You'll be in my care as Lynne returns to work after her maternity leave.

This year has been extraordinary if nothing else. Lynne was promoted, my first book was published, two of my stories were included in "year's best" anthologies. But nothing has been more enchanting or satisfying as Lynne's pregnancy. She and I have grown closer, and our marriage is

strengthening with the impending growth of our family. We
now eagerly anticipate the exclamation point for the year,
the miracle of your first cries.

Chapter Six

12 November

Fifteen years ago on this date, around seven in the evening, in the Ninth-Avenue location of Yamato Restaurants of Pensacola, Florida, Lynne and I ate shrimp and vegetable tempura, drank plum wine, and swallowed belches over giggles, doing our damnedest to be sexy and appealing and loving. Then I slipped a gold ring with a three-quarter carat sapphire stone onto her finger, and we became officially engaged. Later that night, we sealed the promise with more than a kiss.

No seals today—kisses or otherwise. We are both recovering from some rather nasty bugs that put us down for several days. A persistent and bothersome cold caused Lynne to run a constant low-grade fever for several days while I battled the flu for a few days more, my temperature topping out at one hundred three and eight-tenths degrees. At that point, I lay in bed with a pounding headache and swollen sinuses, vacillating between freezing and burning. The flu began last Wednesday with what I thought were allergy problems—a stuffy nose and sneezing—but, as the day wore on, the "allergies" grew worse. By Wednesday night, the bug had burrowed its way deep into my chest, and my head felt as though someone had inflated an oversized lead balloon inside my skull. Thursday night would prove the worst time of all, with my temperature climbing to its highest.

That's the day Lynne's cold set in. By Friday, she was running a one-hundred-point-four-degree fever which made us both concerned. A fever could initiate dangerous conditions for you, so she immediately consulted the doctor who prescribed bed rest and mild cough syrup. While she was at the office (this is the first checkup of any kind I've missed simply because I was too dizzy and nauseated to drive, and, in that condition, it would have been foolish and irresponsible to expose all those pregnant women to whatever virus I had), the doctor checked you out as well. Your heart rate was up to one hundred fifty-eight. The next checkup will come this Friday.

Today is the first day we've felt like doing anything other than lying on the couch or in bed. I cannot recall the last time a flu or cold had me down this completely. With Lynne weathering a slight cold so close to your predicted arrival date and us being firm believers in Murphy's Law, we feared that you would make your debut over the weekend when neither of us was physically ready for you to come. In fact, I would not have been allowed in the delivery room because of the health risk I would have posed to you. But you stayed put—sort of. You've apparently moved lower in the uterus, which means you've begun to "drop" toward the gateway to the new world, albeit a world less inviting than the one you're in now.

Recall that I mentioned I had written some poems concerning the pregnancy and you? I completed them last week as the bug began to attack. The first poem concerns Elizabeth's reaction. The last two—well, you read them:

Severed (for Elizabeth)

No regrets,
she bragged after he died:
I do what I want and to hell with everyone
        else.
Father and daughter in their silence, eternal,
well beyond the grave.

And now it comes to turns and terms,
when wishes aren't what daughter
had in mind, but are prime
to draw the circular glare,
trumping the sympathy play
as she hurls silence
at the next generation.

No thanks.
She settles in her chair, in her room,
television blaring, and sucks Godivas,
recalling when less
scripted voices
filled this house.

Desire

The results show normal
in all areas checked, but we know
they couldn't test for everything—
not enough money, not enough time,
not enough probability.
And positives would require decisions.

The hospital's said to be the best,
at least in this area,
and when you've got little else
to choose from, you take the ward tour
with the appropriate ooos and ahhhs,
knowing, but certainly not admitting,
that cash could get you better.

The classes are straightforward,
no promises, only more probabilities
quoted by a woman who's worked
both sides of the table.

(And mothers seldom understand
when the loss is yours alone.
They crave first words,
to act as relater,
their own tears more important, somehow,
never mind the years, the planning,
the crib, the paintings on the wall.)
This rented movie is nothing,
a shoot 'em up, can't trust anyone flick.
Her stomach's lopsided,
part of us shifting again,
and tears flood her eyes.
"I just want it to be okay."
I can offer no guarantees—
just a shoulder
and a head full of probabilities,
half-steps short of reality.

Lump

At this point, It
is a squirming knot of meat
riding up on her right side,
like a baseball or fist or tiny heel.
And a friend asks,
"Why, in today's world?"

"To give" comes to mind,
but, rather than an answer,
the words sound
more like justification.
What will It determine
between womb and stone?
That life is a dance,
psychotic and malleable?
Or an endurance test,
rewards too few?

As I read "Desire" to Lynne before our colds got us down, tears came to her eyes as the words began to stick in my throat. I still can't answer Andrew's question, "Why have a child?" but I am convinced we've made the right choice. How can I be so sure? Watching Lynne's abdomen grow as you develop, hearing your heartbeat, feeling you move—I just can't give you a definitive answer, but I *know* it's right for us.

Not many more days now, kid, and I'll be addressing you by name in these writings. A wonderful and strange new adventure is about to begin for you and for us. Lynne has a week and three days left to work before Thanksgiving week, the period the doctor now predicts with more certainty as your probable arrival time. Lynne's counting the days, waddling off to work each morning and dragging in each evening as I prepare dinner to collapse uncomfortably on the couch, fidgeting and short-of-breath, wishing she didn't have to go into the office the next day.

In the meantime, you're now playing peek-a-move with the camcorder. Each time I attempt to tape your movements, you stop as if you know. Still toying with me, aren't you? That's okay. I've caught a couple of your somersaults on film, and I plan to catch even more before your debut.

14 November

Today's Ann's birthday. We wired flowers and a wish for happiness in the year to come. With the doctor's give-or-take prediction that delivery might occur around

Thanksgiving, I was concerned you would arrive today, but, to my relief, you didn't. You should have your own special day, not one shared with a living relative.

"Dropping," if in fact that's what's happening, has caused Lynne new and potentially embarrassing problems. Although she seems to be breathing easier as pressure on her lungs decreases, she's losing control over other parts of her body as the pressure points shift. With the cold, she developed a nasty, hacking cough that continues to nag, occasionally causing her to gag and vomit. Last night, she barely made it to the bathroom sink before she did the projectile bit. Unable to control herself from the increased pelvic pressure, she also began to urinate. I found her hunched over the sink, alternately vomiting, coughing and peeing, cursing and crying. I kept my mouth shut and fled before she knew I was there. Saying something at a moment like that might have prevented you and me from ever meeting.

She shouldn't have to endure the discomfort for much longer, according to one of our pregnancy guidebooks. After "dropping" begins, the book says, delivery follows within two to three weeks, which coincides with the doctor's calculation.

My father called yesterday, excited that time is drawing near. He's only eighteen years older than I, but he dons the demeanor of an old man—unless he's riled. Our relationship today is far better than it used to be. During my childhood, especially after he and my mother divorced, we were not close like many fathers and sons. I had always been afraid of him, mainly because of the way he treated my mother. As far back as I can remember, their arguments regularly escalated to battles with her screaming accusations of unfaithfulness and him resorting to his fists. The free-for-all fight before the final in a long line of separations proved the worst and most damaging to us all.

The argument began in the living room of our small, four-room house—over what, I can't recall. Probably accusations regarding his drinking or womanizing or arriving home late from work. They shouted at each other until he threw his hands in the air and fled. Mom followed him into the yard as he tried to leave, then physically blocked him from getting into the car. An uneducated and volatile man with limited knowledge of alternative responses in such situations, he struck out, pushed her backward into the car and slammed the door across her shins, but luckily broke no bones. Inside, according to Mom, although I can't recall, I collapsed, screaming in a fit on the floor.

Mom and I moved two days later to Pensacola to live for several months with her sister and brother-in-law until she could afford a small apartment for us. I was twelve. I didn't like my father then. I viewed him as a cruel and savage man, a view that Mom fostered with tales of heavy drinking and womanizing, of a man who knew nothing but evil. As I grew older, though, I discovered there were two sides to the story, that Mom wasn't exactly Snow White herself. She too had been involved in an extramarital affair—but that does not justify Dad's physical abuse. Nothing justifies a spouse striking out physically against the other. I pledged at an early age that I would never, under any circumstances, strike my mate. In all the years Lynne and I have been together, I have never come close to hitting her, never even thought of it, no matter how heated the arguments.

A lot of time has passed since the divorce, and with it Dad has mellowed and matured, recognizing his own limitations and overcoming them. Over the last ten years, he's suffered some desperate hard times—a faltering business and bankruptcy, the near failure of his current marriage, the deaths of close friends, relatives, and his father—but he's on top now, a successful businessman, happy with himself and satisfied in his marriage. He has earned my respect, and I have earned his. Although we disagree on a multitude of subjects, from religion to politics, we can at least discuss those differences amiably. I am his only child, and his excitement over your birth is understandable. While he is "Paw-paw" to his second wife's grandchildren, you will be his only blood related grandchild, which, rightly or wrongly, guarantees you a special place in his heart.

But no one's more eager or more anxious about your impending arrival than Lynne and I. While we've enjoyed the wonder of pregnancy—the changes in her body, the sound of your heart, the ultrasound images, even the discomfort and inconveniences—we're ready to move on, as you probably are too. What will you look like? What kind of baby will you be? Quiet or complaining? What will you think of us in the years to come? Will you regret your conception? Or rejoice in life?

16 November (2:30 p.m.)

It's another Saturday, and Lynne's finally sleeping on the couch where she's been lying awake most of the day. Don't let her current comatose appearance deceive you. The sleep has been hard won over her concern for your safety. And I'm worried too. The doctor made a disquieting discovery yesterday during the weekly checkup.

That nagging cough and occasional vomiting has caused her to strain or pull a muscle in her right side just below the ribs, the same area where you have lumped throughout the pregnancy. We could never figure out what part of you rose in her side at night, causing her abdomen to appear so lopsided. Yesterday, the doctor showed us. As he checked Lynne's cervix for dilation, he also felt for some part of you in the birth canal. This is the thirty-eighth week of pregnancy, so he should have been able to touch your head, but he felt nothing. He directed Lynne and me to the ultrasound room. The nurse jellied up Lynne's belly. A few moments later, the doctor pointed to the screen and said, "Got a slight problem." He traced the scanner across her abdomen, pointing to the screen. "Here's the head; here are the feet." Your head's rammed under the ribcage on the right, your feet on the left. You're lying transverse. The pregnancy books we have devote only a few sentences to the subject because the position this late in pregnancy is rare. Only four-tenths of one percent of all pregnancies are transverse.

Yesterday's examining doctor, one of several in the practice but not our assigned gynecologist, provided us with general information about the position, explaining that you should by now be head-down, ready for the final thrust out, that dilation of the cervix should already have begun, that the transverse position suggests possible, if not probable, operative delivery. He scheduled another office visit for Monday when our primary physician will return and provide us with more specific details on the position and what it means to the birth.

While he scanned you with the ultrasound, we saw you move, so you're at least viable, but we knew that by the way you rear your head up at night. Your heart rate was strong at one hundred sixty beats a minute. I asked the nurse if the picture revealed your gender, but she said she couldn't be sure. She said the bet in the office is that you're a girl based on—you guessed it—your heart rate. She printed a wonderful profile view of your face which will serve as the initial photograph in your first-year book.

Now, it's wait and worry. Time is dragging by. It has not been an easy pregnancy for Lynne—the basic worry every expectant mother experiences, the physical limitations, the stress of her mother's childishness. Because of her age and the two miscarriages, we've always known she runs a higher probability for delivering cesarean, but now it looks as though the delivery will prove even more difficult than we anticipated. And here I sit, typing notes to an unborn child into this computer, helpless to do anything to relieve Lynne's pain and concern, unable to ensure the safety and health of either of you. I can only reassure her, hold her hand, caress her when she needs comfort. But, if you believe the prevailing opinion of husbands, of men, I shouldn't feel anything, at least not so profoundly, right?

While Lynne has watched movies and read to pass her day, I've cleaned the car in preparation for your ride home from the hospital. Tonight we'll view another movie, and I'll string my guitar with new strings. But no matter what we do, no matter how we distract ourselves, you are constantly in our thoughts as we wonder what the next step will be.

The upside to this predicament, I suppose, is that we may be asked to choose your birthday. You may take your first look around at this world as early as Monday or Tuesday. Then again, it could be three weeks from now. One possible option we may have, the stand-in doctor explained, is to have you physically manipulated into the correct birthing position, a procedure that would prove uncomfortable, painful, and somewhat dangerous to both Lynne and you. He warned us emphatically, though: At the first sign of contractions, Lynne should go directly to the hospital. If she begins to dilate with you in the transverse position, the umbilical cord could fall out, and that could kill you.

18 November (7:30 p.m.)

Monday. Lynne is packing an overnight bag for the hospital, just in case you decide to come before they say you will. This afternoon at the doctor's office, your heart rate was one hundred forty-four beats a minute, showing no signs of distress, but you were still in the transverse position with your spine and back lying across the birth canal, lessening the possibility of exposing the umbilical cord if dilation begins tonight.

At 7:30 a.m. tomorrow, Lynne will check into Humana Hospital's labor and delivery where our primary physician will attempt to physically manipulate you into the head-down position for a vaginal birth. The procedure involves risks. The umbilical cord could be pinched; the placenta could be torn from the uterine wall; labor could be begin. All eventualities would require immediate C-section delivery. If no complications arise, and if the doctor cannot manipulate you into the proper birthing position, then an operative delivery will be scheduled for later in the week. On the other hand, if he successfully turns you, you'll be delivered when you decide you're ready, which will probably be within the next two weeks.

I'll prepare all electronic and camera equipment tonight as though you will be delivered tomorrow. Two still cameras, the audio tape recorder, and the video camera will go with us, but I'll use only the still cameras during the manipulation procedure.

Although we believe our doctor has everything under control, there's the unsettling and real possibility that something will go wrong. Throughout our lives, it seems, we've earned happiness the hard way. Our courtship, our careers, the pregnancy, and now the birth. You think I'm experiencing self-pity? Perhaps, but, for once—this time— we'd like to experience a little gain without the pain.

19 November 1991

After five minutes of heavy duty pushing and twisting, our doctor, the only doctor in Huntsville experienced in the procedure, slipped you around into the head-down, ready-to-go birthing position. He placed the odds that you would remain in the correct position at sixty percent. We'll take another ultrasound look at you this Friday during the regularly scheduled office visit—that is if you don't decide to stick your head out and say hi before then.

I rose at 4:00 a.m. today, unable to sleep as usual, and did my daily jog. Lynne was up by the time I returned, awakened by the vomiting of one of our two cats. Why do they *always* choose to vomit on the carpet or furniture instead of the bathroom or kitchen floors? We dressed and were at the hospital shortly before 6:00 a.m.

Around 8:00 a.m., the doctor began the turning procedure. You should have seen you; at least, you'll see the photographs. You looked like a large Planters peanut with a thin sheet of pale rubber stretched over you. Such a bizarre procedure. Throughout, the doctor reassured Lynne and me with complete confidence that the delivery would go off normally, but he instructed Lynne to head for the hospital at the first sign of any abnormality, including decreased fetal movement or water breakage. So far, some five hours after the procedure, everything looks good.

While we were at the hospital in the large labor and delivery recovery area near the nurses' station, the nurse who conducted the birthing classes we attended stopped by (she works in a private practice and was at the hospital with her employing doctor to assist in a delivery). She expressed amazement to our doctor that he would even attempt to turn you into the birthing position. She pelted him with questions about the procedure: Isn't it dangerous for both mother and child? Don't most turned babies revert to the transverse? Why run the risk of turning? He grew visibly uneasy, especially when she suggested that transverse babies run a higher risk of physical and mental abnormalities, such as deformation and retardation. From where he sat at the nurses station a few feet away from Lynne's bed, he glanced at me, and I simply shrugged. If it were not for the amniocentesis results, Lynne and I would probably be hysterical now with worry, thanks to that nurse.

21 November 1991

A nurse from our doctor's office phoned and asked us to come in today for Lynne's regular checkup because the attending physician will be out of town tomorrow during the time of her original appointment. We've been worried that you may have flipped back into the transverse position, but the checkup revealed your head is still down, right where the doctor put you Tuesday. Your delivery, though, may still be a couple of weeks away because dilation of Lynne's cervix has yet to begin.

Lynne has now decided to go on maternity leave even earlier. She made yesterday her final day at work. She's become far too uncomfortable and easily exhausted to continue a normal work schedule. Everyone at her office wished her well, but, more, they wished her a quick return. She's the fourth person in her office to become pregnant in the last two years. The other three quit after their maternity leave expired. Her supervisors are afraid that she too will resign, but our situation is a bit different from the other women who quit. Their husbands were engineers with regular and sizable incomes. I am a freelance writer, with more free than dollars in the lance. Lynne will return to work, rest assured.

We are undecided at this point whether to inform any of the relatives about your transverse position. We're afraid it could be used as an excuse to ignore our wishes and show up unannounced.

25 November 1991

Still no indication that you'll be here within a week or few days, even though the earliest predicted due date, November 23, has come and gone. Could it be that Lynne's uterus is a far more desirable place than a crib?

If Lynne slows down any more, it'll take her an hour to move from the kitchen to the bathroom, and in her condition, slow movement to the bathroom is not desirable. Each time she rises, her hand goes immediately to the small of her back as she waddles along on her quest to get somewhere.

We aren't sure what's happening with you at this point, but we should have a clearer picture Wednesday, November 27, the day before Thanksgiving, after a scheduled visit to the doctor. Meanwhile, we are doing little more than reading and watching bad movies to pass the time.

Mom, I discovered over the weekend, has been experiencing severe money difficulties with her business (she operates a distributorship of snacks); she's even explored the possibility of filing bankruptcy. The lawyers she consulted told her she'd be making a mistake at this point, that her creditors would probably work with her through the downturn in sales because she has such a good record. So she has begun to "work harder," she says, handling all operations alone while two trucks sit idle and the third, the one she personally uses for deliveries, occupies repair shop space more often than it's on the road.

26 November 1991

During one of our first visits to the doctor, I asked if we could use a standard stethoscope to detect your heartbeat. No, said the nurse. All it could pick up, she said, would be gurgles from Lynne's stomach and bowels.

Last night as we felt and watched you move hither and thither, though hither and thither has become more restricted since the attending physician turned you head-down, I pressed my ear to Lynne's abdomen just below her navel. And what do you think? Yes! I heard your heart beating. I looked up at Lynne, shook my head in disbelief, pressed my ear back to her abdomen, counted the beats at one hundred forty-four per minute. I checked Lynne's pulse—sixty-eight. All without a stethoscope!

I attempted to record the beat with a portable recorder, but the microphones—built-in and extension— were not sensitive enough to pick up the sound. Then you shifted before I could try the stereo recorder's more sensitive mikes, and all I could hear were gurgles and burbles. But what a rush! Thank you so much for such a thrilling moment. What a wonder it's been seeing you grow, experiencing the physician visits with Lynne, feeling you move, hearing your heart, anticipating . . . .

When are you going to poke your head out and introduce yourself?

THE FIRST YEAR

Chapter Seven

What Lynne believed to be nothing more than bowel cramps early yesterday morning continued throughout the day, and, by 8:40 p.m., when she mentioned them to me, the pains had not eased despite several trips to the bathroom. Although the cramps were mild and irregular, their persistence suggested they were anything but bowel related pains, probably early labor contractions. Shortly after 9:00 p.m., she began to spot blood, the definitive sign that her body and you had decided time for action had arrived, but the blood scared the hell out of us. Shades of miscarriage.

Lynne called the doctor on duty for our attending physician who told us the spotting was a normal occurrence in early labor and that we should monitor the contractions through the night and come into the hospital only if they became regular and strong or if her water broke. Otherwise, he told her, come in (this morning) for her regularly scheduled appointment with the primary physician.

At 10:45 a.m. today, Lynne's doctor entered the examination room where Lynne and I waited. He glanced at Lynne's abdomen and frowned. "I'm going to knock a knot on that kid's head," he muttered. To the nurse: "Take her back to the ultrasound room. I want to make sure about this, but I'm pretty sure without it. That kid's flipped back into transverse." The ultrasound pictures confirmed his suspicions, showing that you had not only returned to transverse but had nearly twisted fully around into breach. Breach would have been better. He instructed us to go straight to the hospital where he would attempt to turn you head-down again. Since Lynne had begun to dilate and had entered early labor, he explained, he would turn you, if possible. Then he would break Lynne's water, speeding labor for a vaginal birth.

At 12:18 p.m., the doctor entered the labor and delivery room where Lynne was waiting on a narrow gurney, jellied up her abdomen, and got down to the job at hand. But you, you determined bugger, would not budge. He tried for more than a half-hour, sweat rolling down his face, arms quivering as he strained to turn you, then he sighed, sat on the bedside.

"Won't budge," he said to Lynne with a shake of the head, "which doesn't leave us with much of a choice. As the strength of your contractions increase, there's the risk they'll break the baby's neck. And if dilation continues, which it will, the umbilical cord could fall out. Either way it would be catastrophic." He glanced at us and said, "Are y'all ready to have this kid? We can go into the labor room right now and take it out."

Lynne looked over at me; I nodded agreement. "Let's go," she said. Luckily, we had brought Lynne's overnight bag and our cameras just in case we didn't make it home from the exam.

The nurses prepped Lynne and instructed me that I would be allowed into the delivery room after the surgical cut had been made, that I should stay at the head of the gurney once I was allowed in. "By the way," one of them told me, "you won't be able to have sex for about six weeks or so." I grinned at her. Sex? What's *sex*? We haven't had intercourse since March. What's six more weeks?

At 1:10 p.m., Lynne's doctor began the incision. By 1:25 p.m., I was in delivery, snapping away with both cameras. But you refused to come out! Shortly past 1:30, the doctor began to curse under his breath. He glanced at me, then muttered to the nurses, "We have to get this damn kid out right now." Then he began to cut again, this time up the right side of Lynne's uterus where you'd lodged your head. What he'd expected to be a routine lateral C-section now became a complicated lateral and vertical C-section as time grew critical for your and Lynne's safety. An hour later, he explained to me that Lynne will never be able to have a vaginal birth as a result.

At 1:37 p.m., the doctor sighed, "Finally," and pulled you out by the heels. I stared in awe as he handed you over to one of the nurses. I held one camera in my hands, the other hanging around my neck, both silent at chest level, then I realized what I was supposed to be doing and began to shoot rapid fire, the auto-advance whining. I don't know if I was able to catch any part of you while you and Lynne were still connected by the umbilical cord; I simply shot. I leaned down and whispered to Lynne, perhaps a little disappointed but thankful you were okay, "Your rubber baby boy is here." A shield below her neck prevented her from seeing the operation or you upon delivery. Then I straightened and saw that I was wrong. That blue, rubbery little baby wasn't a boy after all, but a girl.

The nurses quickly wiped you clean and ventilated you, and you fired up those powerful little lungs, your skin pinking up beautifully. You *are* beautiful, Becca. You have wispy auburn hair and a hairline similar to Lynne's. And you have her lush pouting lips and button nose. Faint, brown, fuzzy hair covers your ears, back and shoulders, hair that will eventually rub off.

Becca, you are gorgeous.

The nurses showed you to Lynne, and I was able to photograph her initial reaction, her tears of joy, then I got a tight shot of the two of you, your faces nuzzling each other. The nurses then handed you to me to carry to the nursery. A neonatologist, who had been standing by in case of problems with you, walked with me to the nursery, draping an arm around my shoulders, saying, "She's beautiful, isn't she? Feels different now that she's here, doesn't it?" He had a gift for understatement. I was trembling with feelings of inadequacy.

I photographed all the nursery procedures, from your official weighing (six pounds, thirteen ounces) and measurements (nineteen inches long), through the bath and dressing of your navel. I then returned to labor and delivery where Lynne's doctor was stitching Lynne back together. A few minutes later, a nurse brought you in for a short visit with Mom.

After Lynne spent nearly two hours in recovery (with you there most of the time), the staff transferred her to a private room where she breast-fed you for the first time around 6:00 p.m. At 8:00, I phoned local friends and acquaintances and a couple of Lynne's coworkers to announce your arrival. I called only one relative, Dad, before I left the hospital for home to shower and feed the cats. At 10:00 p.m. from home, I made one other call, to my friend in Australia.

I've decided to forego calls to other relatives tonight. Elizabeth, Ann, and Lynne's sister and her family are on their way to Texas to spend Thanksgiving with Ann's sister, so they can't be reached tonight anyway. Besides, Lynne's not up to talking to anyone, and I'm exhausted, even though I can't sleep.

It's 11:35 p.m. I'm seated at the narrow writing table in Lynne's hospital room. I'll stay here with her as you board across the hall in the newborn nursery until time to go home. The nurses will bring you in for a visit around midnight. I wasn't here when you last visited, but you didn't stay long anyway. Lynne had just vomited when they brought you in, and, since you were asleep, the nurse decided you could wait until midnight for your feeding. I peeked in at you at the nursery a few minutes ago; you were sleeping soundly as other babies wailed.

We've been so eager for this part of the journey to begin, having grown tired of the inconveniences of advanced pregnancy, but now that you're here and Lynne's facing at least six weeks' recuperative time, I feel extremely inadequate and overwhelmed by the job that lies ahead. You're no longer a shifting lump under the skin, a novelty to feel at night or to draw cooing comments in the grocery line. You're a living, breathing, crying little person who depends on us for every whim. With a cat or dog, if the responsibility grows to great, owners can simply give them to someone else; not so with children, at least for most parents. Lynne and I *owe* whatever comfort we can provide to you simply because you had no choice. It is our duty to provide you with the best we can and to stand by you, supporting you in good and bad times, helping you develop into the best person possible. Are we up to the job? It's a little late to be asking, isn't it?

Hospital staff call me "Dad," but it doesn't register until they call me by name. What is a "Dad"? I know what a Dad is *not*. I've known countless biological fathers who are nothing more than names and figures of authority in their kids' lives. I want to be—I *must* be more than that. I want to be a friend, a mentor, a person you can trust and depend on in all matters. I don't want to be the old guy you fear or hate because I'm so dogmatic in my own beliefs and rules.

Becca, I am so thrilled to have you and Lynne sharing my life. Even before the pregnancy, we wanted a child who would be strong-willed, an individual. If your refusal to remain head-down is any indication, we got our wish. I hope you'll have a long, healthy, joyous life. You're embarking on a wondrous, perilous, exciting, and ultimately sad adventure. Maybe Lynne and I can help make the good times even better, the bad times bearable. You have already enhanced our own lives in ways that words cannot express.

I never believed in miracles until today.

Welcome to the world, Becca Fouquet. What a joy it is to meet you.

28 November (8:55 a.m.)

I'm in the hallway outside Lynne's room, seated on steps young children and short adults climb to peer into the nursery at newborns like you. Nurses are bathing Lynne at the moment, and they asked me to wait out here. The window's closed, so I'm sitting here alone.

This morning, I phoned various relatives with the news of your arrival. The first call went to Paula and Dana Barr, who could be your "Mom" and "Dad" if Lynne and I die. They were overjoyed with the news, extremely concerned about Lynne and her condition after such a difficult time. Paula's voice broke with emotion when she related that Rebeccah would have been the name of their own daughter had they not had sons.

I made other calls, receiving a lecture from Mom on how to call Elizabeth, to be kind and forgiving and agreeable. I made no response, but, now that you're here, no one should expect us to change our wishes or plans concerning you. I called Ed and Katrina next, then Elizabeth and Ann in Texas . . . .

29 November (6:08 p.m.)

Sorry I had to break off so abruptly yesterday. The nurses had finished with Lynne and the cleaning woman had finished with the room. After that, the day sort of bled away as I helped Lynne shift in bed, use the bathroom (she can't douche without help at this point), walk to the door and back to the bed for exercise. And you came in a few times, so I never got back to the notes.

As I write now, you are lying in bed with Lynne, wavering between fussiness and sleep after having finished a meal of breast colostrum and bottled glucose water.

As I was saying yesterday, I made a call to Ed and Katrina after talking to Mom. Ed had called our house the night before, on your birthday, and left a message on the machine, wondering if the "turkey is still in the oven," but when I called Thursday morning with the news that the turkey was done, he'd gone fishing with his father-in-law. He . . . .

I'm back now. You were lying beside Lynne when your face abruptly wrinkled and reddened and you appeared to be choking. Lynne broke into tears as she bolted forward, straining her stitches, holding you up, crying, "What's wrong with her? What's wrong?" I took you, placed you face down across my lap. You coughed, caught your breath. Then I lost mine.

Your face had become so red because you were straining to get out your first bowel movement, that sticky brown stuff called meconium. Lynne and I both broke into tearful laughter as I removed the diaper and held it up for her to see.

As I started to say earlier, Katrina took the message that you'd been born, congratulated us, and said she'd call the few relatives that had not made the trip to Texas for the holiday. Then I made the call to Texas.

Ann's niece answered. I related the basic details of your birth, then heard Elizabeth in the background squeal her delight as the niece must have shown her what she'd written. I wonder how Elizabeth will react to the difficulty of the delivery, the danger you and Lynne experienced. "Do you want to talk to anyone else?" Ann's niece asked.

"No," I replied. "But please let everyone know that we won't be accepting visitors until Lynne has recuperated."

Why did I refuse to speak to Elizabeth? Why didn't I use the opportunity to attempt reconciliation? I was exhausted and short-tempered, and I believe reconciliation is now Elizabeth's responsibility, not ours. I had not slept the night of your delivery because I was so excited by your birth and so unnerved by the job that lies ahead. By the time I made the call to Texas, I had been up some thirty-three hours straight. Since I have lost respect for Elizabeth because of the pain and unnecessary stress she's caused Lynne, I did not want to risk a shouting match.

Last night, Lynne began exercising by taking slow trips down the hallway, holding my arm for balance. Today she'll walk the hallway twice. She showered today, and that picked up her spirits considerably. Along with her pain, she's been slightly depressed since the delivery, a common response, so I'm told. At this point, trips to the bathroom are an ordeal. She urinates into a plastic measuring cup, douches with Betadine, and, when she defecates, she has to take careful aim to miss the urine measuring cup that fits over the toilet's front, but the one aspect that makes the bathroom experience embarrassing is that someone must be with her—specifically me; having a stranger, a nurse, to assist her would prove even more embarrassing for her. Despite the compromise in privacy, she's doing well physically. Already she's had two bowel movements, so she was able to begin eating solid food today. The doctor on rounds this morning said that all her vital signs look good, that she and you might go home tomorrow. Knowing how much assistance she'll need during recuperation, it's a good thing I work at home. The wives of men who work outside the house aren't so lucky. The new dads don't have the luxury of long parental leaves that companies regularly provide to women. A case of sexual discrimination, perhaps? Like changing tables only in women's restrooms?

While Lynne spent the day dozing and moving in slow motion, I ran errands and bought this week's various publications such as *Newsweek* and *Time* magazines, both of which came out on your birthday even though they're dated December 2.

You'll hear most of your life that women are the emotionally volatile gender, but I'm not so sure they have a corner on the market. While men might learn to hide their emotions more readily than women, they experience joy and frustration and sadness and humor just as deeply as women, and, many times, they can't mask it. Today, I've been an emotional wreck. Each time I've thought for more than a few seconds about your birth, what you and Lynne went through, what could have happened had the doctor not delivered you when he did, I've had to blink away the tears.

1 December (4:00 p.m.)

Home!

Lynne is reading a book on breast feeding as I write, and you are lying in a bundle of blankets on the couch between us. But that's not the only bundle we're dealing with. Lynne's been a "bundle of nerves" since we arrived home from the hospital yesterday.

4:38 p.m.

Lynne needed assistance in setting up to feed you. She likes to prop several pillows certain ways on the couch to situate you conveniently for her breasts. You're suckling, unaware of the tension Lynne's experiencing from that simple act.

As I was getting to earlier, Lynne's emotions have gone haywire since your birth, and that has possibly hindered milk letdown. As tension adversely affects the production of milk, causing you to suckle harder and longer for less and less, you grow tired and frustrated and must be satisfied with five percent glucose water, which further upsets Lynne, creating more tension, further hindering letdown. We both fear you aren't getting the nutrients your body requires.

Now that you've arrived, we've returned to the care of a family physician who has a nurse practitioner in charge of the children's health program. Lynne called her earlier with questions about letdown and nutrition, and the woman assured her you're doing okay, that Lynne only needs to relax and the milk will come. But if it doesn't come in by Wednesday, she said, we can replace the water with formula designed specifically to supplement breast feeding.

Last night, Lynne could not sleep. She still finds the bed uncomfortable due to physical limitations, so she has moved to the couch as she did during the last weeks of pregnancy. But now I too have come to the living room to sleep so I'll be readily available to assist her or you. Around 3:00 a.m. last night, Lynne lost all emotional control as you tried to feed. She sobbed indomitably with worry that you aren't getting what you need. I comforted you with glucose water and tried to comfort her, reassuring her that milk letdown would occur eventually, that you would be fine, that babies are notoriously strong, but she simply had to cry the emotions through. The depression that began in the hospital is persisting. Maybe after Wednesday, after either her milk comes in or we supplement your feedings with formula, maybe her demeanor will improve. But Wednesday seems like an awful long time from now.

As for you, besides the problem with breast-feeding, you're having slight, but normal, hormonal problems—specifically, vaginal discharge of blood and mucus. (Could hormones be contributing to Lynne's depression as well?) And you haven't had a bowel movement since we left the hospital, but that too is supposed to be normal. After all, you aren't getting much more than the glucose water during feedings, so there isn't much, if anything, to be digested. The day before we came home, you became slightly jaundiced, That too, our family physician said, was a normal reaction of your body to its new environment.

All this normal stuff scares the hell out of me.

2 December (9:48 p.m.)

I picked up the photographs of your birth today (they're wonderful, Becca, simply wonderful), but when I returned home I found Lynne in tears. I dropped to my knees, took her hands as you lay in her lap, whispered, "What's wrong?"

"She's got dried milk all over her mouth," she said. She wiped one cheek dry. "There wasn't much," she said, "but at least it's starting." Maybe, maybe this means her spirits will improve.

We gave you your first at-home bath today, and you did not enjoy it at all. I washed you with a bath cloth and shampooed your hair as Lynne, still convalescing from surgery, watched and directed from the toilet.

Life is refusing to settle into any semblance of routine, hectic and unpredictable, but it will get better as Lynne's health improves and chores are once again shared. At present, she concentrates on feeding you and resting while I take up the slack—changing you, bathing you, cleaning house, cooking, caring for the cats, and on and on. It will get better.

9 December (8:46 p.m.)

You're feeding again. Over the past week, you've settled, more or less, into a three- to four-hour feeding schedule, but your night habits leave a lot to be desired, mainly sleep. Each day, you feed, you look around, you go to sleep. Around 1:00 a.m. daily, you wake, slightly hungry, feed for a few minutes, then keep yourself and us awake until 6:00 a.m. or 7:00 a.m., crying. You feed again, then sleep. Lynne's still worried you aren't getting enough milk because there's no way to gauge the amount of milk coming from the breast.

We're running on empty. On Thursday night, for instance, Lynne suddenly broke into sobs of desperation and confusion, worried whether you're getting enough nourishment, and worried about her ability to keep up with your demand, worried that we made the right decision to have you.

One day after I phoned the doctor's office with concern that you had not had a bowel movement, you filled your diapers five times, all normal, so sayeth the nurse practitioner. As for your fussiness, perhaps it's related to a desire to suckle but not feed, but you refuse to have anything to do with pacifiers, preferring instead one of our fingers, and even that doesn't satisfy you at three in the morning.

I've busted butt this week to finish the pregumentary, staying up until 2:00 a.m. Sunday through Thursday only to rest an hour or two before rocking and walking with you while Lynne sleeps. Although I'm not ecstatic over the end result, the video will have to do because I had to get copies out to relatives as promised. Last Friday morning, I mailed copies to Dad, Mom, Carol, Paula and Dana, and to Elizabeth and Ann. I wonder if the emotion and sheer miracle of you on video will touch Elizabeth. Neither she nor Ann has acknowledged your birth.

I see you've finished feeding. Time to belch, squirm, and, perhaps, (please!) sleep.

11 December (10:40 p.m.)

I'm seated on one end of the couch writing as you sprawl sleeping on Lynne's chest on the other end. We took you in for your first medical checkup today, the two-week checkup, and, frankly, it has us worried because it bore out Lynne's concern that her body isn't providing you with enough milk. While all your reflexes proved normal, your weight left much to be desired, specifically seven ounces. You were down to six pounds, six ounces from your birth weight of six pounds, thirteen ounces, what you should have at least weighed today. Some loss during the first week is normal, but not through the second week. The nurse practitioner, a La Leche breast-feeding fanatic, instructed Lynne to feed you every two hours or on demand, whichever came first, but Lynne is doing that already. She's plugging her nipples into your mouth at least every two hours, and you feed upwards of an hour or more each time. The practitioner said the prescribed schedule should get your weight up by next week when we take you back for another check.

My question: If that kind of feeding schedule hasn't sustained you yet, why should it by then? I asked the practitioner if we should begin supplemental feedings of formula as she suggested earlier, but apparently she's had a change of heart. She said she recommends only increasing the frequency of breast feeding further. To what? I wonder. A tit in your mouth at all times? So I asked what would our doctor recommend.

"Probably supplemental feeding," the practitioner said, but the best milk for a baby is its mother's milk." Agreed, but some mothers can't produce enough. Lynne appears to be one.

It doesn't matter. If you don't gain weight by next week, we begin formula feeding—to hell with the practitioner's fanatical dedication to the mammary glands. You are far too precious for us or some nurse to risk your health on the "in" thing.

After the checkup and spending nearly two hours in parking lots at the doctor's office and the University of Alabama for Lynne to breast feed you (we won't drive without you strapped securely in the car seat), we stopped by her office where you met about ten of her coworkers. You even smiled at her supervisor, but I don't believe he smelled the reason, a diaper soaked with green poop.

For the next couple of weeks, until your eating needs are adequately met, Lynne's only responsibility is to feed you on the two-hour schedule. Everything else falls to me, but I don't mind. We have to get you to the weight you're supposed to be at. But if breast feeding fails, changes will be made. You should not suffer, not when alternative nourishment is so readily available.

14 December (10:09 p.m.)

As of 4:30 p.m., you are a formula-fed baby. For the past week, especially the last couple of days, Lynne has done little more than bathe herself and feed you as you suckled for hours on end. Over the last forty-eight hours, Lynne has slept perhaps six. The two-hour feeding schedule never materialized. After each feeding, you'd cry for more within thirty to forty-five minutes. Feedings lasted an average of three hours. Physically exhausted and unable to gauge your intake, Lynne has become increasingly depressed and ill-tempered as her nipples have grown ever more tender. Frustration has mounted from lost sleep, your occasional inability to latch on, and the pain from sucking That frustration has certainly affected milk production, which hindered your ability to feed, which bred only more frustration. Two nights ago as I lay in bed listening around 3:00 a.m., I heard her strike the couch again and again in anger and pain as you suckled at her breast.

Today, tearful and exhausted, she asked me to go to Wal-Mart and buy a can of formula. The decision came after a short telephone discussion with the practitioner who implied that I, as a man—and all men are the same—had not been doing my share to assist Lynne, that Lynne, if she could "only hold out" for a couple of more days, would have a rewarding, fulfilling experience as a mother and as a woman.

Yeah, right. Get a life, lady. Had she seen the look of satisfaction on your sleeping face after you downed your first four ounces of formula—had she seen the relief in Lynne's eyes as Lynne watched you drink—she might have realized that fulfillment is a matter of perspective.

A Christmas card, the first acknowledgement of your birth, arrived for you today from Elizabeth, signed "Your *grandmother!* Your mother's *Mom!*" Apparently the game continues.

As I watch you lying in your crib or as you suckle the bottle while I hold you, I feel at such a loss, so completely inept as a parent. I want to protect you from the world, from the poison that will destroy your innocence. If I had the power, you would never know grief or anger, loss or mistrust, envy or jealousy. Like any father for his child, I wish you great joy throughout life, and, if it is within my power, I will help you obtain that joy. Lynne and I are charged with the responsibility to foster your growth as a good person, to help make your journey as enjoyable as possible. You, on the other hand, owe Lynne and me nothing more than the respect we show you. Live your life in the manner that brings you happiness, and we will rejoice with you.

18 December (10:03 p.m.)

After suffering through—no, *enduring* a few evenings of fussiness and an inability to soothe you with food or walking, we purchased a wind-up baby swing. You are now zonked out, swinging back and forth, cutting a few million Zs after having gulped down a couple of ounces of formula. And speaking of formula, today you weighed in at the doctor's office at six pounds, eleven and a half ounces, and you've grown a half inch. We could not have been more pleased or relieved. The nurse practitioner, who appeared more supportive today of our decision to formula-feed you (perhaps because the doctor came in to check you personally), instructed us to keep you out of crowds and away from anyone ill to avoid possible infection. Seems there are some nasty bugs going around. You return for your one-month checkup on December 27, then again in January (if nothing causes us to carry you in sooner) for the first in a series of immunization shots. Also today, the remainder of your umbilical cord fell off. Looks like you're going to be an "inny."

Carol phoned this evening to check on your health. She said Elizabeth is still steaming over our "seclusion" during these first weeks, that she has no intention on "making up" with us. That news hasn't helped Lynne's depression any. Even the good news about you today has done little to pull her out of what is growing into a severe postpartum funk. Whenever I suggest she talk to the doctor about it, that it may be hormonal in nature, she snaps, "It isn't *that*! We just need time to adapt." Adapting to our new lives may be part of it, but not the major part. I've never seen Lynne like this, and I don't know what else I can do to make it better for her.

The days and hours since your birth have become a haze of diaper changes, feedings, walking, and rocking. Next week is Christmas, as if you could care. My good friend, Andrew, will spend the day with us. He's even bringing the ham. Maybe that will cheer Lynne some.

Soon we'll be raising a toast on video to you. (We've been unable to do it prior because of breast-feeding restrictions, the fact that you would consume alcohol in the milk.) And we'll be taking your "first Christmas" photograph with you stuffed into a stocking Carol made for you—which will probably become one of those embarrassing pictures we'll pull out to show your friends in years to come.

23 December (2:08 p.m.)

You're draped face forward over my right arm as I type this entry. Lynne's running errands. (I finally convinced her to get out of the house, away from you and me, to do something, anything, on her own. I hope the time away will brighten her mood some, but, she's sunken so low, I doubt one day's shopping will do much to improve her outlook.) You haven't felt like sleeping since last feeding nearly an hour ago. Lying on your back's no fun right now, and neither is your swing. Seems the only thing you're interested in is watching my fingers working the keyboard. That's fine with me. I like holding you, but over the last few days, being held has proved little comfort to you in the afternoons and evenings. You've begun to experience severe gas pains, and though you pass gas and burp, it apparently doesn't relieve the pain. We put a call into the nurse practitioner earlier today for advice, but she has yet to phone back.

Your bowel movements have begun to settle, and you're down from five-plus movements a day to one or two, apparently common for formula-fed infants.

We have returned to bed to sleep now, but, during the first days when we were sleeping on the couch, you would sometimes sleep on Lynne's chest, sometimes on mine. One night, Lynne called out my name, wanting me to take you because you needed a diaper change. I shot up, coming out of sleep and a dream, my arms cuddling you to my chest until I realized you weren't there. I panicked, fearing I had dropped you. That's one of the few times since coming home that Lynne has smiled.

8:40 p.m.

The nurse practitioner finally called and suggested that a change in formula brands and types could solve your gas problems. I hope so. We can feel the gas as it bubbles through your intestines. Each time it rumbles, you cry out in pain.

By the way, Lynne is still moping, sighing, and staring into space. What can I do?

You know, Becca, despite the continuing two-hour feeding schedule that goes through the night, despite the endless changes of diapers, mixing and heating of formula, despite the endless walks up and down the hallway to calm you, despite all the time-consuming and frustrating things infancy requires of us, I would not have it any other way. You have made me feel more complete, that my life somehow has more meaning. And yet I still can't answer that question, "Why have a child?"

24 December (9:20 p.m.)

You're quiet now after a couple of hours of fussiness caused by gas. We've bought a medicine we could give you to relieve the pain, but the nurse practitioner says you're too young, even though the directions on the package say the medication is perfectly safe for infants your age.

Lynne has been baking today in preparation for Christmas. The baking is a good sign. In the past, she has used baking as a type of therapy. Maybe . . . .

With each of your feedings tonight, Lynne and I will exchange one gift, then exchange the rest tomorrow morning.

28 December 1991

Just a quick entry. You now regularly slurp down several ounces of formula each feeding, and, yesterday, the nurse practitioner informed us it's paying off. You weighed in at seven pounds twelve ounces, and you've grown to a length of twenty-one inches. The only problem you're having is the gas, usually in the evening, but we're going to try the medication I mentioned in an earlier entry. The practitioner was wrong about breast feeding; perhaps she's wrong about the gas reliever. In two weeks, you'll begin immunization shots; two days later, after Lynne's six-week checkup, if all is well, we'll head south to Pensacola to introduce you to the relatives who wish to meet you.

Later today, I'll install a couple of rear speakers in the car. If I don't destroy the car, after your last evening feeding, I want to play guitar for a while before bed. Lynne insists on getting up during the night feedings now, so we've begun to trade off feedings, one playing an instrument while the other feeds you, but I use the guitar as Lynne uses baking, as therapy, and I've become rather short-tempered myself in the last couple of weeks. Maybe *my* hormones are rebelling now. Maybe I can coax them back to their normal levels with a few gentle chords.

29 December (11:15 a.m.)

Remember that gas problem I mentioned? Both you and Lynne are now asleep in the living room—her on the couch; you in the playpen—after a long night of gas and crying. This morning, with you screaming with gas pains, we gave you a dose of the gas relief medicine, a simethicone solution. It worked, if your sleeping is any indication. You've been asleep since nine this morning.

Lynne tried to soothe you throughout last evening until she allowed me to take you at 1:00 a.m. I fed you, but you continued to cry until falling asleep around 4:00 a.m. on my chest as I rocked you. I attempted to put you in your crib once, but you began to cry again. You soon dropped back to sleep as I rocked you again. I rocked you for two hours until your next feeding. After that, you began to cry again, so we gave you the medicine, and it provided relief.

It's a gray, chilly day, overcast and wet. And I'm tired, but I still have work to do. Yesterday, I installed rear speakers in the car (turned out great, much better than I expected), washed clothes, cooked dinner, cleaned house, and mailed out several manuscripts. Today, I have a short story to complete and more housework. How does the saying go? A woman may work from dusk 'til dawn . . . ?

I now have a t-shirt that displays the photo of you and Lynne I took a few minutes after your birth. Underneath, Lynne has written in small letters the word "birthday" and the date.

I had a dream about you a couple of nights ago. Lynne had carried you in her uterus as long as she could, but you still needed to stay in another month. So doctors physically altered me to carry you to term, but you would not stay put. Gray and bloody, you kept popping out of my chest until Lynne said it was okay, that it wouldn't hurt if you came into the world early.

Lynne's depression continues, and we're both touchy, snapping at each other over such stupid things as how we hold you. Perhaps our intolerance is due to fatigue and in part to the pending trip to Pensacola. I've read more on postpartum depression the last few days, and most of the authors agree that after a baby "settles," the mother usually emerges from the depression. But "settling" could take as much as six months!

Friends and relatives warned us that pregnancy would be the most difficult part, but they were wrong. These first few weeks since your birth have been extremely trying and difficult. I feel at a loss, unable to cheer Lynne and much of the time unable to cheer you. I find myself sinking in the process. I try to imagine the future, conversations between you and me, a time when Lynne and I are once again normal and not at each other's throats. If I could only convince her to consult the doctor about the depression . . . .

31 December (6:50 p.m.)

Last day of the year, and what a year it has been. Lynne's promotion, a published book, and you. Most of all, you. Although the nurse practitioner has officially declared your nightly crying as "colic," which could last for months, I would not go back to the life we enjoyed before you arrived, not now. You represent a challenge, and I know we can succeed. We simply must try harder.

Lynne's funk continues as she rides an emotional roller-coaster. She can be relatively level and even pleasant one moment, then accidentally tip her glass of water on the table, and suddenly she's snapping at me, crying for nothing. That's one reason I believe it may be hormonal in nature, the suddenness of mood changes.

Next week, you'll receive your first immunization shots, which will make you grumpy for a couple of days, and that should make our Pensacola visit even more memorable since those grumpy days will be spent there.

It's colic time. You're crying in the living room with Lynne. I should close now to relieve her. In an hour or so, we're going to sip some peach wine and munch Chinese take-out. Afterward, we may reflect on an amazing and fabulous year, one that spawned such a precious jewel. Or maybe we'll just claw each other's eyes out. In either case, we are so thankful you have come into our lives.

Happy New Year, Becca.

Chapter Eight

5 January (9:10 p.m.)

You're still on the every-two-hours feeding schedule until further notice from the doctor, but you've gotten to the point that you're no longer hungry every two hours. Lynne's in the living room now, attempting to feed you, but your stomach's too full of gas for you to eat. We believe the gas problem may lie with your formula, which has a cow's milk base. If lactose intolerance is the problem, refusing to eat now may alleviate the gas pain, but then you'll be hungry, we'll feed you, and the cycle will begin again. We'll call the doctor tomorrow for an okay to switch to a soy bean-based formula which has no lactose.

This afternoon, Lynne again took some time away from home and us to enjoy a few minutes semi-alone: She went grocery shopping while I stayed here with you, trying to calm your screams by walking the hall, bouncing you, patting you, rocking you. Finally, you wore yourself out, falling asleep for only a short ten minutes. Then the screaming began again, and continues now, intermittently. If a change in formula doesn't alleviate the gas, we'll have to look for some other cause. I don't believe the answer is as simple as "colic," and I don't believe you must suffer this way. Yes, I know. Every other new parent has probably said or thought the same thing.

Despite the colic or restlessness or whatever it is, Lynne's depression appears to have eased some since she no longer has to feed you each time you're hungry. Those marathon feedings wore her down, especially those that dragged out through the night. I now do the night feedings, but she'll still take one or two on occasion. When she returns to work in February, I'll be doing nearly all feedings, day and night.

Wednesday you go in for your first immunization shots, which may cause grumpiness for a day or two. On Friday, we'll travel to Pensacola where Lynne will confront her mother at some point. Elizabeth effectively prevented baby showers before your birth, but Paula Barr and Carol have decided to give her one anyway now that you're here. It will be held at Paula's Saturday.

I'm looking forward to introducing you to Paula and Virginia and to two old friends, Ken, one of my best friends from high school, and Isabel, a former coworker. In '82, I worked as her teacher's assistant in a class for mentally handicapped young adults. I learned a great deal from her example, including patience and tolerance. By watching her and listening, I learned how to step out of myself in many situations to view a situation through the other person's eyes. I've attempted to do the same with Elizabeth, but I've failed so far. Perhaps it's because I'm too close to the situation, having witnessed the unnecessary pain she's caused Lynne. Isabel is a special person. She possesses a wonderful gift of understanding and caring I hope you'll possess in years to come.

7 January (4:30 p.m.)

Some good news! We changed your formula yesterday to a soy bean-based brand. You slept soundly all night and most of this morning, crying only when you were hungry or uncomfortable. And today's bowel movements were exceptionally good—soft and easy to pass compared to the lumps you've been dropping the last couple of weeks. We're keeping our fingers crossed that you'll be comfortable with the new food, that your "colic" will end with this change. But then, six o'clock is still two hours away, and that's when the nighttime howls usually begin. Tomorrow is immunization day, so rest well for now.

8 January (3:35 p.m.)

You've had a hard day, haven't you, kid? Hang in there. Visits to the doctor will get easier in time, trust me.

You now weigh eight pounds, ten ounces and measure twenty-three inches in length, and you were doing so wonderfully—calm, smiling—until the nurse practitioner began her prodding and boisterous attempts to reassure you that she meant no harm. Then she brought out the needle and dropper for the oral immunization (Grab the jaw, squeeze open the mouth, squirt it in: "Down the throat, child, now swallow!"). You screamed your discontent while I swallowed mine. Your visit today was supposed to be a quick check and shots, but instead the practitioner decided to perform your two-month checkup ahead of schedule. Your next visit will come in late March when you return for your four-month checkup and another round of immunization shots. Whether we change doctors is yet to be determined. I don't care for the practitioner. I believe she allows dogma to cloud sound medical judgment, and I loathe her loud and arrogant bedside manner.

On several occasions, we've asked the practitioner about this or that aspect of your well-being. Each time, her response has been the same: "That's perfectly normal for babies." While whatever we're unsure about may be "perfectly normal," the questions posed are those we can't find answers to in the books or literature we have on hand or in the library. I would like a bit more explanation and reassurance than the snappy "perfectly normal." If we went in and said, "We noticed Becca's hands fell off during the night," I bet she'd respond, "That's perfectly normal. They'll grow back soon enough, you'll see."

Tomorrow, Lynne's gynecologist will either pronounce her perfectly normal or perfectly abnormal. But, if she checks out okay, then Friday we'll be on our way to Pensacola.

At the moment, Lynne and you are asleep on the couch. The change in formula has apparently worked, at least for now. The gas pains you were experiencing have lessened, and you're resting better. The usual colic time last night was considerably shorter with far less crying and squirming. I hope it continues. We feel so helpless and useless when you suffer for no definable or treatable reason.

It's winter in north Alabama, which means perpetual gray has set in. It's raining now. I shouldn't complain because I usually thrive on rainy weather. But for the last month, it has rained more days than it hasn't (nearly a foot of water for the month); and on the days it hasn't rained, the clouds have remained. Drab days don't help much when you're depressed, but Lynne's begun to fight back. She's doing better. I have known her twenty years, but I have never seen her as depressed as she has been the last few weeks, not even after her father's tragic death in '72. While the weeks preceding your birth proved one of the most wonderful periods in our lives, I can say without reservation, these weeks following your birth have proved the most difficult time in our marriage. She has sunk into such spiteful moods, snapping or moping, despite all my efforts to please her, to relieve her from household duties other than feeding you. I'm not saying I've been perfect. I've become tired and short-tempered as well, and I've reacted in anger too many times to count. No matter how much rest she has, how much less she has to do, she remains in a funk, although, as I said, it's grown better over the last few days. Maybe the trend will continue.

9 January

Lynne just called from the gynecologist's office. You and I stayed home to avoid anyone with colds and to allow Lynne some free time away. You've finished your mid-morning feeding, and the formula is agreeing well with you so far. Your stool is soft, and you're resting better. Lynne said the gynecologist gave her his blessings and sent her on her way. She can return to a normal life, which means she'll be exercising again, something she's wanted to do for the last couple of weeks. She gained a lot of weight during the pregnancy and hasn't been able to lose any since your birth. That's been one ingredient in her depression, so maybe exercising, dieting, and weight loss will help her.

She'll eat lunch out and do some browsing and shopping before coming home, then we'll ready ourselves for the trip to Pensacola tomorrow. I'm not looking forward to it. I dread the confrontation that will surely come with a face-to-face meeting with Elizabeth. It shouldn't be this way. Our relatives, especially our mothers, should be rejoicing in your birth, the fact that you are healthy and doing well after a shaky start. We all live as though we're immortal, as if time places no limits on our lives and relationships, but time eventually runs out on us all. Isn't it too precious of a commodity to waste on such childishness?

15 January (6:30 p.m.)

What was I saying? Something about wasting time? The trip to Pensacola has ended, but its effects will be with us for some time to come. Conflict, collision—what a weekend!

We stopped first at my father's on Friday. Dad and his wife, Martha, live in a small town north of Pensacola. He was so proud of you, grinning and gushing, showing you off to strangers and friends and relatives alike. He babbled on and on about how beautiful you are, how much you resemble Lynne (we can't see any resemblance to either of us). Shortly before we left, he nodded at me and said, "Let's take a walk." We walked out to the pond behind his house. He pulled out several bills from his pocket, shoved them into my palm. "That's for Becca, for her college or whatever," he said. A couple of hours later, I counted $400, all of which has been placed in a bank account for you.

We arrived in Pensacola at Paula and Dana's around 5:00 p.m. You were fussing and hungry, so Paula took you into her arms, speaking softly, cuddling. She fed you, rocked you, calmed you. Lynne attempted to contact her mother by phone, but Elizabeth and Ann were out, Carol later told us, treating their neighbors to dinner. She tried several times throughout the evening, then again on Saturday, each time without success.

We went to Virginia's, where you met my mother, but you began to cry each time Mom held you. After the first time, she would preface picking you up with "now let's see if I can make you cry."

Although Elizabeth didn't show at the baby shower that Paul and Carol gave on Saturday, she sent a message to us via Carol. Lynne and I, she'd told Carol, must "take the next step," which I assumed meant that she expected us to apologize for having requested time alone with you. Lynne said nothing in reply to the news, but the depression I thought she had begun to shake settled in once again. After all, she's attempted several times to reconcile in an adult manner, but Elizabeth refused to speak with her as you know. Elizabeth's a hard woman. Despite the pregumentary video we sent to her and Carol's and Paula's efforts to act as mediators who related the difficulty Lynne and you experienced during late pregnancy and delivery, Elizabeth refused to give up the assumed role of victim. Yet we tried again.

Sunday morning, Lynne, you, and I arrived at Elizabeth and Ann's unannounced. Ann answered the door, surprised to see us, invited us in without the usual hugs. Elizabeth looked around from her easy chair and rose. I was behind Lynne, carrying you. "Do you want to meet your granddaughter now," Lynne said to Elizabeth, "or after we have a talk?"

Elizabeth glanced at me, then back to Lynne. She did not look at you. "After," Elizabeth said, and she turned abruptly for the bedroom.

Ann remained in the living room with you and me. I had brought two mini-albums of photographs of the birth and the weeks afterward to show all relatives and friends. I handed them to her, and she flipped through quickly, skipping most of the pages. She laid the books on the couch between us. "I suppose y'all are going back home today," she said.

"We'll go back Tuesday," I replied. "Lynne just wanted to come out here today to talk to her grandfather's daughter."

Ann's face went cold at the reference to her husband and his stubborn nature. I admit, the comment was out of line. She rose without a word and went into the bedroom where Lynne and Elizabeth were talking. I followed her to the doorway with you in my arms. "Excuse me," I said. All turned toward me. "Do you want both of them in here?" I said to Lynne. The odds were a bit lopsided, but she said it was okay.

Lynne was superb. She maintained an adult and calm tone throughout, staying on track despite Elizabeth's efforts to divert her from the primary issue, Elizabeth's reaction to our request for privacy. Elizabeth and Ann at one point laid blame for the situation on me, pegging me as the "instigator" by writing the "scathing letter" that demanded they "stay away from the baby forever."

"I have a copy of the letter in my purse," Lynne said. "Nowhere does it forbid you from visiting or seeing Becca. In fact, let's take it out right now and go over it line by line."

Elizabeth refused. All references to the letter ceased. At one point, she attempted to insult Lynne by saying that "you've always been *different*," but Lynne only smiled, accepting the comment as compliment.

After the "talk," Elizabeth held you and fed you for about forty minutes. At one point, she wiped away tears and said to you, "You don't like your milk, do you? You don't like it at all." Whether it was a dig at Lynne's inability to breast-feed, I can't be sure, but I do know it hurt Lynne, rekindling feelings of failure.

Two hours later, we drove to Fort Walton Beach and over the toll bridge to Santa Rosa Island, checked out a parking lot in search for a place to watch the Gulf from the car while we fed you, but the parking lot didn't provide a good view of the water. We pulled back onto the road, signaled to turn left into another parking lot, stopped in the lane as oncoming traffic passed. The car behind us stopped. A moment later, our car lurched forward with a crunch. My head flew backward, sinking into the headrest. You began to scream.

The car came to rest on the road's shoulder. I twisted around. Lynne had already begun assuring me that she and you were okay, just shaken. I got out, checked the car, found the rear folded in for a good twelve inches. The car behind us had damage to both rear and front, the front windshield cracked from the driver's head as she was thrown over the wheel. In the car behind hers, a sixteen-year-old boy and his fourteen-year-old girlfriend sat calmly, watching me as I examined the damage. The boy's car had rammed the middle car, driving it into us.

Three hours later, Lynne, you and I were released from a local emergency room. I had suffered minor whiplash while you and Lynne had been shaken slightly. The doctor warned us that your appetite may decrease for a few days due to stress. Our car, on the other hand, will require major surgery. I meet with the adjuster next week to ascertain damages, repair costs and reimbursement for out-of-pocket medical expenses.

18 January

As the emergency room physician predicted, your appetite has decreased considerably over the last few days, reaching its lowest point yesterday. After midnight, though, you began eating more. You've been having some bowel cramps today, causing discomfort and crying.

You've now lost most of the hair you were born with to the point that you resemble Winston Churchill. Just put a bowler on your head and a cigar in your mouth.... The hair on your back and shoulders has rubbed off as well.

After the wreck last Sunday, Lynne and I were sitting in the car—she was in the back seat, holding you, as I sat in the driver's seat—waiting for the State Trooper to arrive. At one point, she handed you up to me to hold. I nuzzled my cheek against yours. Lynne leaned forward, touched me lightly on the shoulder. Neither of us could stop ourselves from crying.

25 January

I've spent most of this week wrangling with the at-fault driver's insurance company. Our car's frame is bent, and the insurance man has hinted that he doesn't want to pay anything beyond the basic cost of repair—no medical reimbursement or loss in the car's value (placed at $1,000 by the dealership where we bought it).

You have improved, though. Your appetite has returned and you're active. Yesterday I placed you in a chest carrier, facing forward, as I worked. You enjoyed watching my fingers on the keyboard and the images flickering on the monitor screen. I hope your cooperation continues after Lynne returns to work next week because I am far behind in my own work.

Lynne remains off-center emotionally—depressed and something more, but I can't put my finger on exactly what "something more" is. I've suggested before that her emotional state may be hormonal in nature, but she continues to refuse that as a possibility. Maybe the situation between us and Elizabeth is bothering her more than she admits. A friend of mine said it took his wife nearly a year to overcome her postpartum depression. Oh boy.

I've completed a lullaby for you. It was originally an instrumental until I added words to the end.

"Time waits for no one.

"Don't spend too much trying to make it last.

"Time waits for no one.

"In the blink of your eyes, the future has passed."

27 January

Last night at 2:30 a.m., I set up the video camera and recorded your lullaby while Lynne fed and rocked you. During these last few days before returning to her job, she has been rising for nearly every nighttime feeding. I'd like to stay in bed and sleep, but I'm afraid she might resent me for it or grow angry, so I keep her company, usually by playing guitar until you've finished eating.

I wonder if the age difference between you and me will make our relationship better or worse, of if it will matter at all. When our parents were the age we are now, Lynne and I were seniors in high school. We'll be fifty-three when you're eighteen. Will two old codgers straining to hear the same old rock-and-roll bother you, or will you want to crank up the ancient Tull and Beatles albums to enjoy the beat with us?

I'm back after having stepped over to your room to watch Lynne change your diaper as you kicked happily on the changing table. The couple two houses north of us gave birth last week to a girl they named Morgan. They don't realize how lucky they are. When the woman first discovered she was pregnant, she celebrated by going on a three-day drinking binge. And she continued to smoke throughout the pregnancy.

To drive, one must pass a proficiency test and be licensed. To fish, the person must be responsible enough to be licensed. To fly, practice law, practice medicine, to hunt, to operate a business—they all require certain proficiency and licensing. But anyone who has his or her sexual gear in working order can become a parent. What if people had to complete training to obtain a license to have children? What if we had to pass basic proficiency tests in parenting? Would there be fewer unwanted and abused children? As much as Lynne and I prepared for you, we were unprepared. But what about those who celebrate pregnancy by getting drunk, by continuing to smoke, by doing what they know is wrong and potentially damaging to the fetus? What kind of parents will they be?

I hear you crying, and Lynne's tired, so I'll relieve her now. Next week, she returns to her job.

30 January

Lynne and I have just exchanged apologies for yet another misunderstanding. About two hours ago, you became inconsolable. Lynne, frustrated and angry, placed you in your swing to let you cry it out. I suggested we all "go for a walk," but I didn't wait for her to reply before taking you out of the swing. Lynne thought I was insulting her or suggesting she wasn't capable of parenting properly. She felt hurt and snapped, "Just go by yourself." I walked out with you, too angry to say anything. When we returned, Lynne explained how she felt I'd overruled her as a mother. I told her I'd only been trying to quiet you, not to insult her.

The friend whose wife suffered the postpartum blues suggested that all we need to do is get in the sack and go at it. The doctor's given us the go-ahead for sex, but who's in the mood? It isn't like we're sixteen with those let's-do-it-in-the-hall hormones knocking around between our thighs. We're too tired or too angry, with spontaneity apparently a thing of the past.

Sex. It's been nearly a year. You're in your room on the floor with Lynne now, a string tied loosely to your ankle with the other end tied to your mobile so you can make it jiggle, but you've begun to cry again. She's untying you, and I hear the rocking chair creak as she settles to rock you.

You're nine weeks old, approaching the magic point when your attitude is supposed to improve, according to all the books I've read. If what you suffer from is truly colic, as the nurse practitioner insists, it should let up around the twelfth week. But the books warn it could drag on for as long as six months. Won't that be fun?

Chapter Nine

3 February

Lynne returned to work today, leaving you and me for our first full day on our own since your birth. What do you think so far? A little more attention to detail, perhaps? I agree.

For nearly a half-hour this morning you screamed. You weren't wet and you didn't seem to be hungry. Each time I tried to feed you, you would take the nipple into your mouth, suck a moment, then spit it out, screaming even louder. I rocked you, I walked with you, I sang to you, I tried feeding you again, to no avail. Then I checked the bottle's nipple. Why hadn't I thought of it earlier? The holes were clogged. A new nipple solved the problem and quieted you immediately. Since then, it's been eat, sleep, wake, change, eat, sleep . . . .

I figured that I'd get little work done because feeding you requires both hands, but I've contrived a way. I place you in your infant carseat, roll a blanket into a cylinder, lay it across the carrier over your chest, then place the bottle on the blanket at an angle to your mouth. So far, so good. I can work at the computer while you drink and watch.

You've finally begun to grow hair. It looks as though it will be dark auburn in color, about the same as Lynne's. Whether it'll be curly like mine or straight like Lynne's we can't tell yet. It's little more than a Marine cut at this point.

Tax season is smothering finances once again. Used to be kids didn't need a Social Security number until they reached the teen years, but now the government requires everyone to be tattooed by age two. Why? An attempt to make more money by closing loopholes, I suppose—taxing kids' incomes and interest on bank accounts, that kind of thing. But that doesn't matter, really. Because of you, we'll net a return this year instead of the usual "pay-more." And soon we'll apply for your Social Security number.

What's the latest in the relative saga, you ask? Mom says that had your birth come at a more convenient time for her she would have reacted in the same manner as Elizabeth. Since Mom had other commitments, she "didn't mind so much." As for Elizabeth and Ann, no word from them since our trip.

6 February

Our car is in the shop for repair, but the insurance company continues to balk at reimbursing us for loss of value and cost of medical treatment. The entire rear panel of the car has to be replaced, from the back window on. It should be completed in a couple of weeks. I suppose that's when we'll do further battle with the insurance people.

These last three days with you have been wonderful. We rise around 7:00 a.m. You eat, play, sleep, then do it all over again several times throughout the day. I hope this is a sign that you're "settling," that the colic is over, and that you aren't experiencing a deceptive calm before some dark and terrible storm.

Lynne also is doing better since she returned to work, the postpartum blues apparently are beginning to fade. This weekend, we will go on a family outing, first to a bookstore then to Burger King. This is the first time we've done much of anything away from home since your birth, not counting the trip to Pensacola. We've been reluctant to take you out during the cold season, but the house has become too stifling. We all need to get out more together and enjoy each other's company in different settings. Perhaps

it will further alleviate Lynne's blues and decrease my own grumpiness.

13 February

The family outing of errands this past Saturday went well but slow. By mid-afternoon, the majority of errands still lay ahead, so I brought you and Lynne home, then returned to town to finish them. Amazing the speed you can accomplish errands without having a little one along.

My mother's birthday is today. You and I called her this morning, waking her, to wish her a happy day. She referred to you as "Me" as in "How's *me*?" She hasn't called you by name yet, always some saccharin term of endearment.

Here are a couple of items in the news recently: First, a survey of graduating high school kids across America suggests that fully one-fourth cannot read well enough to locate the expiration date on their driver's licenses. Another survey suggests that girls and boys enter school with the same potential and abilities, but due to teacher favoritism toward boys in math and science, girls do worse in those subjects and show lower self-esteem as they progress from grade to grade.

Don't be fooled by surveys, Becca, and don't be led by anyone. You can buck the odds by being anything you want to be because you're as good as the best and better than the rest. Work to please yourself, and you will not be disappointed in the long run. Don't allow anyone but yourself to set limitations. Soar as high as you wish. Be happy and content with your life.

14 February

Your appetite has returned with voracity. I can barely keep up with the demand, bottle after bottle. Some people have told us to mix infant cereal with the formula to "give her stomach something to digest," but I don't believe much in old wives' tales. You receive all the nutrients you need from the formula. When the time is appropriate, we'll switch you to solids.

So, what are you going to be, Becca? Physician, lawyer, housewife, bag lady, engineer, astronaut, musician, writer, seamstress, burger flipper? Whatever you choose, choose for yourself, for your own happiness, but choose carefully and wisely. Then persist and you'll excel, though it may take a long time. Of course, the right partner will help you attain your goals, but ultimately it's up to you. The elements to succeed lie within. Use them.

17 February

Today is President's Day, and Lynne's home because it's a national holiday. After I wrangled for several hours with the insurance adjuster, he decided to approve paying our medical costs from the car accident. Our car is still in the shop, though, and the battle for compensation for loss of value still lies ahead.

Over the weekend, I had some wallet size photos printed for Paula, us, and relatives, including those who no longer admit to being related. I've sent them on their way, but I doubt we'll receive any acknowledgement from Elizabeth or Ann. Amazing the feud has lasted this long— even more amazing that it began at all!

Becca, you are so beautiful. As I lie on the floor or bed beside you, watching you kick and grab at the air or my fingers, I can't stop the tears from coming. We are so wonderfully lucky, so blessed by your presence. When I remember all the things Lynne and I have done together, the places we've been, the adventures we've had, I have difficulty recalling them without placing you in the memories. It's as though you've always been with us. In some way, I guess you have.

You've reached a milestone: You've begun lifting your head while lying on your stomach. Although you quickly become frustrated by the inability to do more, your strength is increasing, carrying you toward the next accomplishment. You've even begun trying to sit up, but each effort ends in defeat and angry grunts and sobs. Soon, girl, soon.

18 February

I've spent much of the morning sorting through the items we've accumulated for your first-year book. Newspapers, magazines, photographs, cartoons, hospital identification bracelets—Lynne will do a spectacular job assembling the book. She has practiced by compiling books for Leigh and Allen, and their parents have enjoyed the books tremendously. But your book will contain a host of materials and oddities that theirs do not. For instance, yours will contain a sky chart for the time of your birth and a tape of that day's National Public Radio's broadcast of *All Things Considered*.

You're progressing as you're supposed to, entering a phase in which you don't sleep as much, especially during the day, fighting to stay awake when you feel yourself drifting off. You fidget and grumble until you wake yourself fully, then you want to be entertained. Sitting in my lap at the computer today, you became enthralled by a screen saver program with its intricate designs scooting across the screen, transforming constantly, bouncing, flashing, disappearing. I spent a good ten minutes watching you watch the images. You leaned forward off my chest several times toward the screen, sitting momentarily unsupported.

You've been experiencing severe gas pains the last couple of days during late afternoon/early evening, which might be due to the increase in formula consumption. Last night, you went to sleep exhausted around 7:30, so Lynne and I also took the opportunity to turn in early, about 8:30. No sex, just sleep. Although you've recently been sleeping up to six hours straight at night, last night you woke at 10:15, hungry and wet. Then again at 2:00 a.m. and 4:45 a.m. Will you please tell me why you choose only week-nights when I do the feedings to be an insomniac? Couldn't you occasionally pick a Friday or Saturday night when Lynne takes a couple of the feedings?

24 February

They always seem real.

You were lying on your changing table while I changed your diaper, a large, open bag of cotton puffs beside you, on my right. In the dream, you had learned to talk even though you were the same age as you are now. As Lynne came out of the bathroom behind me, you asked, "Why are women different from men?"

I laughed. "Lynne will have to answer that one." I turned to her only to find her eyes widening in horror as she glared at you. I spun back around as you sank into the bag of cotton puffs, grinning, waving. I ripped at the bag, des-perately trying to tear the plastic open so you would not suf-focate, but the bag grew ever thicker with new layers. You continued to giggle, your face blurring under the plastic, your breaths growing increasingly labored, the plastic crack-ling around your mouth and nose with each inhalation, but you did not realize the danger as I screamed, "No!"

I sat up suddenly, coming out of the dream, sweat-ing, panting, my heart pounding. I glanced at the clock: 4:00 a.m. I rose quietly, went in to check on you. I placed my hand flat on your back to feel your breathing. I returned to bed, tried to sleep, but it wouldn't come.

We feared the third pregnancy would end like the first two and that we would lose you as well. With the birth, I thought the fear of losing you would decrease because mis-carriage would no longer be a threat, but I was wrong. The possibility of losing you is even more of a fear now because so many dangers exist.

Despite the dream, you're doing wonderfully. You're lifting your head easily and rocking on your belly, complaining and fussing all the while, and you're grasping objects with greater strength. You aren't as fascinated with your hands and feet as the books I've read claim most infants your age should be. You prefer to expend your interest and energy in attempts to sit up. You'll strain and grunt with your feet in the air, your face growing beet red, until Lynne or I help you by taking your hands and gently pulling you up. You then look around as though you've conquered a new world. If we lay you back down, you immediately begin to grumble.

What's next? Who knows? You don't seem to be one who follows the standard line. You've proved you prefer to handle life in your own manner—even back in the uterus when you refused to remain head down.

It's 11:00 a.m. You're asleep in the chair beside me as I work here at the computer. You've slept better and longer through the night over the last couple of weeks, but two days ago you reverted to the two-hour schedule, which has meant less sleep for me. This morning, Lynne fed you when you woke at 5:00 a.m., her normal rising time, allowing me another hour of sleep. According to the books, you're supposed to be sleeping completely through the night. Don't you listen when we tell you these things?

You now weigh twelve pounds. You'll have soon outgrown the infant carrier and will need the infant/toddler carseat. Thrilling stuff, huh? A couple of days ago, I saw a woman in a car's passenger seat cradling her baby, smaller than you, as her husband drove down the street. Two other kids under age seven were playing in the back seat, wrestling and jumping. I don't understand why parents allow their children to ride in a car unsecured, unprotected. Children haven't the luxury of experience to choose to be unsafe; parents should care enough to make sure their kids are protected. Had it not been for your infant carrier, you would have suffered serious injuries in our accident. The woman in the car behind us crashed into the windshield because she wasn't wearing a safety belt. Where would you have ended up? You may cry and complain, but you will *always* wear proper restraints in a car while you're a child. We will not risk your safety. We don't have that right.

26 February

You and I drove to the Social Security office to apply for your number. You should receive it in ten or so days, then we'll open a savings account in your name.

You are becoming increasingly restless during the day, and you're easily bored with the toys I put before you. You prefer instead the sit-up game, grasping my fingers as I pull you into a sitting position, but even that doesn't entertain you for more than a few minutes at a time. All in all, I accomplish about two hours' work each day, if I'm lucky, which means a nonfiction article I'm doing for the state's business magazine is taking far longer than it should. I'll complete it Saturday, maybe, but before you were born, the article would have taken only a day from rough to final draft.

On Sunday, I'll begin building your toy box, which will look more like a hope chest than toy box. It will incorporate the moon-and-star motif to match your changing table.

1 March 1992

You're becoming quite an around-town type of person. Friday, you and I spent part of the day at the annual computer fair and running errands; Saturday, you, Lynne and I went shopping; and today you went grocery shopping with Lynne. You've been wonderful, complaining at a minimum, more interested in watching people, cars, and cans.

Although other people fascinate you, you don't care for them holding you. One of Lynne's coworkers and our next-door neighbor have tried to hold you, but you began to cry immediately. Then there's Andrew. He can take you, cuddle you, and walk you outdoors, leaving us behind, and you don't mind at all. I guess you can sense how much we like and trust him.

A few minutes ago (it's noon, sunny, in the upper sixties), Lynne brought you back to my desk where I was working and told me you'd discovered your hands. You held your right hand before you, fingers curled, and stared quietly at it for several minutes. It appears your next milestone will be the ability to roll from your stomach onto your back. Yesterday, you hiked your leg upward and struggled for a good five minutes on the floor, nearly rolling once, but not quite.

I'll stop it here for now. Before writing this entry, I completed a typesetting job for a high school student. Now it's time to get to work on your toy box.

4 March

Your toy box is in pieces, each cut and sanded, ready to assemble, which I hope to do next Saturday.

As I've mentioned before, I've been recording your sounds since early pregnancy. Yesterday, after changing your diaper, I tickled you as you lay on the changing table. The recorder happened to be within reach as you began to laugh. I then played your laugh on the tape, but it frightened you, causing you to cry, which I also taped.

You've finally achieved another first. Although with great difficulty, you've been able to roll over twice, straining and wiggling from your stomach onto your side, then toppling over to your back to kick, squirm, and gripe because you can't roll back onto your stomach.

Although we can't see it, friends and relatives assure us that you resemble Lynne. Perhaps it's the lush lips or the full cheeks, that Mexican ancestry showing itself. But we are certain you inherited my skin condition—dry and itchy in winter, which means you'll probably keep a lotion factory operating in the black throughout the years.

You're asleep at the moment, your eyelids fluttering with dreams, your breathing rapid, your feet twitching. Two nights ago as I rocked you at 2:00 a.m., you drifted into sleep, grinned, and chuckled.

Chapter Ten

6 March

We've begun measuring time not by our birthdays or national events but by your growth and increasing mental and physical abilities. You've become adept at raising your head to look around while lying on your stomach, but that newly developed ability doesn't stop you from griping. You still have great difficulty rolling onto your back, and you can't yet sit up without help. You've begun to hold your bottle with both hands, but you either can't or refuse to support its weight fully. You also grasp and shake rattles when the mood strikes. You'll shake them back and forth as you lie on the bed under the Mickey Mouse newborn "swing," kicking and squirming excitedly when you connect with Mickey or Donald to make them move.

I should finish your toy box tomorrow. It will also serve as a dressing bench in years to come. I'm looking forward to getting it into your room and storing your toys there. At present, we keep them in a paper bag in the closet.

It's a gray, rainy Friday. I've just completed a short story that'll go out tomorrow, and Lynne is at her office, a far safer place to be than on Huntsville streets when they're wet. You were born in "Rocket City," a nickname purportedly derived from the rocket and space-related companies here, but I believe the name is derivative of the way residents drive.

9 March

This weekend marked a nonstop babble fest for you. You jabbered on and on, as though having a conversation, upwards of a half-hour at a time, whether we responded or not. Even now, you're babbling as you sit in the walker with three squeeze toys arrayed on the tray before you. You can't negotiate the walker yet, but you can move it. You apparently enjoy the mobility despite its limitations.

I completed the toy box over the weekend. Next project? Another bookshelf because our book collection keeps growing, just as our music collection constantly gives birth.

Oh, what's this? Grumpy babbles? Time to slip on my entertaining shoes. What shall I try? "Me and My Shadow"? Or would you prefer simple conversation?

16 March

Whoa! Dodge that squeaking Garfield. Deflect that stuffed Donald. Good arm, kid. You're tossing toys off your walker as well as any major leaguer. Perhaps the first female pitcher for the St. Louis Cardinals?

This weekend marked several milestones. You began puttering around in your walker to points you desired, although you went mostly backward instead of forward. You began passing toys and other objects from hand to hand. And you turned at will from your back to your stomach without much strain.

Out of all the stuffed animals, squeaking toys, and rattles, what would you guess is your favorite toy? A diaper. You thrill in pressing it to your face and growling into it, over and over and over. You've also discovered a means of expressing frustration and anger: You grabbed Lynne by the collar Sunday and gave her what-for, babble style. It's so wonderful watching you develop, your personality and ability defining themselves by the day. Last week we sent our wills to Paula and Dana. The following message was included.

Dear Guardian(s), and Dear, Dear Becca,

The reason you're reading this is obvious: Lynne and C. Steven Fouquet are dead. Before we tripped into the other world, we asked you to open this package only upon our deaths. Dead we may be, but our dreams and desires for Becca live on. We ask you to indulge us this one last time. Some of our requests may seem strange, but then, you know how we were in life, so why should we be different in the afterlife? ("Ah," someone grumbles from the far beyond," get on with it, you morbid goon." Okay, okay.)

In part, this . . . letter . . . is to you, Guardians; in part, to you, Becca. If Becca is under 18, still in her formative years, we hope you, her guardian(s), will respect our wishes in areas we feel (or felt, as the case may be) critical to the development of a well-rounded human being.

We ask you to rear Becca to be open-minded, liberal some would call it, willing to tolerate and consider diverse points of view, to judge people objectively, based strictly on personalities and actions, not on accepted stereotypes.

We ask you to rear Becca with an gentle, but certainly not lenient, hand, instilling the ability to understand and accept responsibility, the ability to forgive as warranted, and the ability to accept change and growth in the ones she loves.

We ask you to teach her to act responsibly to others and to herself, to respect and value friendship and love, to respect herself and others.

We ask you to rear her with an ability to accept blame when rightfully placed and to accept acclaim when earned and deserved.

Above all, we ask you to rear her to respect the value of other human beings, to cherish the gift of another's affection.

And, Becca, please be assured, we loved you more than our own lives. You are our message to the future, but a message that must be written as you see fit—not your guardians, not your relatives, not us, only you. We hope you will receive the best in life, but if you receive the worst, we hope you will be equipped with the strength of character to face it head-on and to overcome.

In some obscure, demented way, we miss you even now, which is to say we miss our own lives. As we write, Becca, you are only thirteen weeks old, a squirming mass of bones, groans and meat whose touch we cherish. We hope we'll be privileged to see you grow through childhood, through adolescence and adulthood, even into your gray years, but if not, we will always be here, either in memory or spirit, to accompany you with each step you take toward the end.

L & C

There you have it. I pray the first time you read these words will be the night we go out to dinner to celebrate your thirteenth birthday when we give you these notes to commemorate your passage into adulthood.

20 March

Yesterday should be remembered for two events. First, and more important, you let go with your first, full-throttle belly laugh, and we captured it on audio tape. You were lying on the floor on your back, and I was gently shaking you by the arms, back and forth, making idiot sounds that you must have loved because you began to giggle, then came the roaring belly laugh that proved contagious.

A week from tomorrow will mark your four-month medical checkup and the second round of immunization shots. And you should begin eating solid foods that weekend, starting with the mush of baby cereal. Yum!

To better accommodate your increasing mobility, I now have a "portable" office. Tuesday, I built a small case with three shelves and wheels to accommodate the computer. I can now roll it into whatever room you're in and work there. So far, it's served well when you've cooperated, but this week, you've wanted to be held more than you've wanted to play on your own. At the moment, I have the keyboard on the kitchen table, clicking away, while you nap in the carrier on the table before me. I thought your growth would allow more time for working, but I accomplished more when you spent most of your day in the baby carrier, sleeping and eating.

Okay. It's time to stand up and cheer. Or at least allow a sigh of satisfaction. After a year of celibacy, Lynne and I have cracked the sex barrier once again. Intercourse was planned last night, but it was intercourse nevertheless. Little in the way of fireworks, but at least the fuse was lit. Maybe sex will improve our outlooks, improve our mutual responses, lessen our argumentative moods. Yes, we're still tired; yes, we're still arguing; yes, life goes on. We're trying to return to a semblance of normality by going out for dinner this weekend, the first time we've been away from you for an evening together since you were born. We'll venture to a restaurant where a host will seat us, where we'll order from a real menu, where the lighting will be muted and sensual—a severe change from the glaring, clamoring fast-food places we've eaten at since your arrival.

All the nit-picking, tiny considerations of parenting, the accommodations, the small questions and worries— there should be some kind of owner's manual that pops out of the uterus with the kid. What were those damn birthing classes for? There should be more—parenting classes required of all couples even contemplating procreation. I've scanned the bookshelves for books about or by fathers like myself, the stay-at-home, primary caregivers, but I've come up with little, only occasional "Doonesbury" strips hinting that others like me *are* out there. Perhaps we should form some kind of national club, a Stay-At-Home-Fathers Anonymous. No. We're already anonymous enough. We need to know each other.

23 March

Saturday afternoon proved a little much for you and Lynne, I'm afraid. Saturday morning, the hives that plagued Lynne through pregnancy last year returned in large patches. You and I accompanied her to the doctor's office where she received a prescription for an antihistamine, but no explanation of possible causes. She was to take the medication and return in two months for a checkup. By the time dinner rolled around, Lynne felt nauseated, and you were crying, so we came home.

This coming Saturday, it's your turn with the doctor. I'm sure you'll be in a wonderful mood afterward, but maybe you'll allow me time to edit your first-year video. I haven't viewed any of the footage since we began shooting. It'll be wonderful to see it all again, comparing you now to you four months ago. What a difference a short time makes.

26 March

Yesterday, you and I met Lynne at the mall for lunch. Afterward, you and I purchased a new stereo receiver and took it home, unboxed it, and began to set it up, but, in the middle of it all, you began to cry and became inconsolable. I thought you might be hungry, but you wouldn't eat. I placed you in the swing, but it didn't satisfy you. Placing you in the walker failed. I laid you on your back, made google noises and faces—useless. I placed you in your carrier, bounced you, held you. Nothing worked. And then I failed.

I held you up before me and raised my voice, begging you to "Shut up, Becca, please shut up." The volume scared you, causing you to cry even harder. I am so sorry, but that doesn't mean anything to you. I failed. No excuse. None at all. I cuddled you and rocked you, blinking back my own tears, until finally you calmed an hour later. What was wrong, I'll never know. I do know that I need some rest, that I need to chill out. I do know that I failed.

It's about 9:30 a.m. You've just finished a bottle, and you're in the walker, alternately gnawing on a plastic chain, a rattle, a Garfield squeeze toy and a large stuffed inchworm. Yes, you've entered that gotta-taste-everything stage.

Next week I'll turn thirty-six. When I was eighteen, I figured I'd know so much more by now, but I still feel eighteen, crawling into Mom's old yellow Mustang to haul ass up 69th Avenue, Alice Cooper screaming from the radio, "I'm a boy and I'm a man . . . ." I thought age would bring wisdom and understanding, but it has bred only more confusion, more uncertainty.

I'll take the day off so you and I, if it's warm, can visit a park where I'll place you in my lap to swing and to bounce on the spring-mounted horses. Then we'll meet Lynne for lunch. In the meantime, Lynne's hives continue unabated as we vacillate in our relationship, from good to ballistic and back. I wonder if she feels like having sex.

Chapter Eleven

30 March

Weight—thirteen and a half pounds; length—twenty-five and one-quarter inches. You're doing wonderfully, according to our family physician. (You won't be seeing the nurse practitioner again. She's no longer on staff. The reasons aren't exactly clear, but the nurse's response implied that few, if any, were sad to see her go.) Saturday, you underwent your four-month checkup and received the second round of immunization shots. Next standard appointment comes in May. You've finally reached an average weight for your length. What great relief.

You began eating solid food yesterday, if you can really call that rice mush solid. You had a blast with the first two feedings, playing with it mostly as we stuffed in small spoonfuls, but today's attempts haven't been as successful. You've already grown bored with it, preferring the ease of the bottle. Swallowing mush is more difficult than swallowing liquid.

You'll help celebrate my thirty-sixth birthday this week, since you've begun solids, by sampling a tiny taste of my cake. The weather isn't going to cooperate for a visit to a park as I'd hoped. The high for the day is expected to reach only the mid-forties, so we'll meet Lynne for lunch at the mall or some fast-food restaurant, then spend the rest of the day running errands.

What will you remember from these early days of life? From my own early childhood, I recall precious little, but snatches persist—scenes, glimpses. In one memory, I am in the front seat of a car, lying down beside Mom. She appears frightened. I assume that scene follows the time I ate a tablet of roach poison I found under the couch. In another snatch of time, masked faces hover over me, a gentle woman's voice telling me "it" will be okay, then one of the masked persons lowers something oval and beige over my nose and mouth and a cloth covers my eyes. Whether the masked faces were connected to the poisoning or to the removal of my tonsils at age two, I don't know. The next scene, I am riding in my father's arms through the hospital parking lot around dusk. A light, humid breeze is blowing. I feel safe in his arms, despite the abuse I've already witnessed against my mother.

The physical abuse and the fights that led to it comprise the most vivid of my early memories. I can hear Mom badgering Dad with questions and accusations as we ride home one night from his parents' home. I see him grab her by the hair and yank. I hear her cry. On another occasion, he's in the bathroom, getting ready to go out "juking," as he put it, my mother accusing him of things I don't understand. I see him swinging, pushing her backward. She falls, he steps over her, disappears out the door and into the car as she screams at him. Whatever you recall of Lynne and me, it will not be scenes like those I witnessed.

6 April

Another milestone reached this past weekend: Saturday you sat up unsupported for almost an entire minute. Then Sunday you screamed from gas pains throughout the night. You didn't eat well yesterday, and we're not sure what the problem is. The doctor suggests it's nothing more than your system adapting to solids. Perhaps you had a slight virus. You appear better this morning following a squishy bowel movement.

You and I spent my birthday shopping in one sense of the word: We didn't buy a thing; we only looked. We met Lynne for lunch at the mall because the weather was chilly with a record low in the twenties the night before. The day following my birthday, we shopped again, this time buying license plates for the vehicles and a couple of CDs and books.

You love paper—looseleaf, books, tablets, whatever. You rejoice in the sound and feel as you crinkle, wrinkle, wad, wet and destroy any paper within reach. The flood, I see, is coming soon as we place books and breakables on higher shelves throughout the house. What does this love for paper foreshadow? That you'll enjoy your homework? Or relish destroying it?

9 April

It's 3:00 p.m., and you're zonked after a ride through the neighborhood on my chest, facing forward in the cloth carrier. We saw a squirrel dart across the road, watched a bee crawl on a dandelion, touched a pine cone, and watched a dying beetle struggle up a stick. You enjoy our daily walks, kicking excitedly from time to time, never griping. I wish I could say the same about your waking time in the house. Here, you gripe considerably (I recorded you earlier today), sometimes for hours. It seems I can't please you at all inside the house. Perhaps when you become more mobile, you'll be more satisfied. You're growing stronger by the day, so scooting and crawling should come soon.

You're doing well on solid foods, eating about six teaspoons a day now, but that hasn't stopped you from waking once each night to feed on formula. Some people have suggested that we should ignore your cries, that you'll go to sleep on your own, that "crying it out" will break you from night waking. I don't think so. If you didn't need at least comfort, you wouldn't be crying. A child must know it can depend on its parents. If we're available every time you call other than when you cry out at night, what will you think of us? Will you trust us implicitly, or will that trust be undermined by our lack of response at night? Next week, we'll add a new food to the rice and oatmeal cereals you already eat. By adding one food a week, we can gauge any sensitivities you may have to particular foods.

Lynne returns to the doctor this weekend for another check on the hives. She's been taking antihistamines for the past couple of weeks, and, though the medication's helped some, it hasn't eliminated the itching or splotching.

I find myself less tolerant and shorter tempered these days. Much of it is due to fatigue from rising with you several times a night and attempting to make life for Lynne as easy as possible, doing most of the housework and child care while attempting to carry on with my career. I find myself more easily ticked with Lynne, but I try to express it in ways other than arguing with her. Take the following poem, for example:

Afterbirth

I am tired of hangers on doorknobs,
of milk dried in bottoms of cups,
of magazines on the kitchen table,
of vacuuming carpets,
of clothes in closet hampers,
of oil draining from cold engines,
of whims,
of dramadies,
of hormones,
of speaking quietly in the morning,
of saying I'm sorry, of being forgiven.

I am tired.

You pat my knee,
tell me the house looks good,
car too,
kiss my cheek,
fall asleep on the couch.
Through the window,
I see the grass is high,
and a load of clothes
sours in the washer.

Remember the nonexistent parenting classes I've ranted that every parent should be required to take before pregnancy? I could have used one or two or three or more of them—especially in tolerance. I become so angry with you sometimes over the most ridiculous things. You cry and cry, and I can't calm you, so I blame not only you but myself as well for my inability to soothe. But crying's normal, a fact I realize, and yet I feel as though I've failed both you and me. I'm doing my best to be a good father, but I don't know what a good father is. I'm learning about fatherhood as you learn about life, Becca. I just don't know if I'm as quick as you.

14 April

Another milestone. You've begun to play interactively with Lynne and me. You'll touch our faces, then place your open mouth on our cheeks or noses or foreheads and growl the way we growl at you. You're propped in the curve of the couch playing with large plastic doughnuts and having a good time. Ooops, there goes the blue ring . . . There. Happy once again.

Someone's switched off winter but forgot to turn on spring, going instead straight to summer. It's in the low nineties today, too hot for this time of year.

Earlier today, you and I were outside when Lynne called and left a message on the machine. When we returned inside, I placed you on the bed, rewound the tape, played the message. When you heard Lynne's voice from the machine, you turned expectantly, so you obviously recognize our voices.

Lynne's checkup last Saturday did little to make her feel better. The doctor suggested that the hives are with her indefinitely. Further treatment will consist of several months of using an antihistamine designed not to cause drowsiness, then, if the hives persist, testing for allergies.

You and I now go for a walk each day, weather permitting. You thrill in watching everything around you, listening to various sounds, and *swimming* in the wind, squirming with your legs kicking and arms flailing. We've blown dandelions and watched bees and ants, stopped to watch and listen to birds singing on nearby tree branches. You've fallen asleep twice, gnawing on my thumb. Yesterday, we all walked to the park where Lynne placed you in her lap to swing.

It's coming on summer, Becca, and I'm slipping into a nostalgic mode, playing certain albums, including "Tubular Bells," "Sundown," "Horse With No Name," "Dark Side of the Moon," and a lot of others I'm sure you'll be tired of by the time you read this diatribe. The summer after I graduated high school proved magical for me, a summer of defining myself and my goals, a time the music helps me nearly recapture. I miss the friends that populated those few months, and I've tried to contact several since then. Most attempts have failed, and those that have succeeded have been disappointing. We've all changed. We've buried the people we were to slip into lives of people we don't readily recognize. We somehow lost the ideals of equality and the possibility of a better world, compromising our principals to make sense of reality. We retreat now to our living rooms or offices occasionally to pull out the old records in an attempt to resurrect that certain innocence we had back then, those feelings that we could make a difference, that our lives would have meaning in the end. Then we put the records away and return to work, satisfied in our impotence, a little sadder with the truth.

You're getting cranky. Tired. Maybe hungry. Time to move on.

19 April (1:22 p.m.)

It's Easter, and this has been your day: Play, grump, eat, poop, pee, sleep. You're asleep now on the end of the couch while Lynne sits in the curve, perusing a magazine. Last night, I remained up until 1:30 a.m. writing a letter to Rick, my friend in Australia. What a guy. He's one of the most talented writers I know, yet his work endlessly searches for publication while he makes ends meet by working for a messenger/delivery service. If anyone deserves recognition and success on pure merit, it's Rick.

Progress report: You sit up easily on your own now, falling over occasionally, and you now enjoy playing with an assortment of toys, entertaining yourself for a few minutes at a time. We bought you a bucket of shapes (triangle, cube, circle) and a double-sided activity center. Both enthrall you when you're in the mood, but your interest is fleeting, transferring quickly from toy to toy.

It's a rainy, cool Easter this year. This morning, I installed child-protect locks on all the cabinets, with adequate cursing and grumbling, but they all work. Mobility is approaching quickly, so it's best for us to be prepared.

Thursday, you and I met Lynne at a riverside park on Redstone Arsenal for lunch to celebrate the twenty-first anniversary of our meeting. Yes, we've known each other that long—and they said it wouldn't last (which only made us more determined). Afterward, you and I bought a couple of CD packages for Lynne—Beethoven's nine symphonies and a single CD of Dave Brubeck containing "Take Five." I would've preferred celebrating with Lynne by having sex, but her personal sex drive is still in low gear apparently.

Friday, you and I cleaned house. You were wonderful, entertaining yourself most of the day while I rearranged furniture, vacuumed, swept, and washed and folded clothes. We began when Lynne pulled out of the garage, and we finished, sitting down on the couch for a drink of tea and munching of Sun Chips just as she pulled into the garage. Are we good, or what?

My mother's been ill. She says a spider bit her, that "I ain't never been this sick before." After a couple of weeks of anti-venom medication, she's better. My dad, on the other hand, has been undergoing tests to discover why blood showed up in his urine during routine medical exams. Possible kidney stones. Possible prostate problems.

Soft, Native American flute music on the CD player, cool breeze through the window, you snoozing, Lynne munching, and I'm yawning. The carpet beckons.

23 April

Yesterday, I edited your first-year videotape up to the present. Lots of wonderful images of you, but, I'll be truthful, it doesn't reveal the difficult time those early weeks presented for us. Those weeks are like the Dark Ages, a time I would not want to repeat. No more infants. If I were younger and less concerned about your well-being, which would mean far less stress, then I wouldn't be so final, but another infant at this stage in our lives would be irresponsible. Don't get me wrong. While it's been a difficult experience that has created friction between Lynne and me, it has certainly been worth your company. No, I don't regret our decision to have you at all. I simply wouldn't want another.

You can now thrust your pelvis into the air while lying on your back. You draw your feet under your buttocks and push up suddenly. And you've been able to lift yourself into a hands-and-knees position for a few seconds at a time. You don't often turn from back to stomach or vice versa, but we know you can. And though the duration is still short, you're entertaining yourself with toys while you sit on the couch beside me during the workday. Of course, you still bore easily, so a procession of toys must pass through your hands, but after a half-hour or so, you demand that I put the computer on hold and play with you.

Last night, you had finished eating by 2:00 a.m. The next feeding, I guessed, would come around 5:00 a.m., which would have allowed me three blessed hours of straight sleep, but at 3:30 a.m., one of the cats began puking on the bed and on the carpet in five separate places. As a result, I've been nodding off all day.

30 April

All right! You slept through the night (more or less). You ate at 9:00 p.m., unusual for you, then slept until 4:30 a.m.. Lynne rose at her usual 5:00 a.m., took you, allowing me to run in the park. I felt like a superman, having slept six straight hours. Perhaps you slept better because you're consuming solids better. The foods now include infant oatmeal and rice cereals, cooked apples, pears, and bananas; next week, Lynne will add peaches. She's sitting on the floor at the curve in the couch where you're sleeping as she manicures her toes. I wonder what she'd do if I slipped over beside her, kissed her, brushed my hand against her breast.

No . . . perhaps it's not a good idea. She just cursed and grimaced and pulled her foot even more sharply toward her waist.

As I mentioned in earlier entries, you're becoming better at self-entertainment, now playing with toys, especially those that make noises, for upwards of a quarter-hour without whining. And your ability to sit without support has improved vastly. You rarely fall over now. You're also vocalizing more, forming certain sounds of speech, but none recognizable as words as yet. Paula and Dana will visit us May 13 on their way back to Pensacola from Paula's father's home in Canada. They're looking forward to seeing you, and they've suggested we leave you with them while we spend the night out to dinner and a movie. We'll probably prepare a meal here and socialize with them since we haven't seen them for a while.

4 May

Yesterday you had your first bout with vomiting and diarrhea, thanks to me for buying and cooking plums for you. That's right. Plums. Prunes that haven't yet dried. You enjoyed them, gobbled them right down, but yesterday afternoon you puked them up, then had one hell of a bowel movement. I am so sorry.

Mother's Day looms ahead, followed soon after by Father's Day. These are two days I do not believe in. Why should days be set aside to honor fathers and mothers whether or not they deserve honor? Those days imply that children owe their parents for giving them life. Not so, not so. Children *owe* their parents nothing but the respect they receive from their parents. It is the parents who are indebted to the children. Children do not ask for life; they have no choice in the matter. Life is a cruel joke that ends with death, and nothing can change that. Responsibility lies with parents to their children, to ensure good lives for their offspring as best they can. If a mother or father is a good parent, they require no special day set aside to say thanks. Every day is Mother's Day and Father's Day.

7 May

A quarter to three, and I've finished work for the day. An overcast, chilly day with a high of only sixty-two and low expected tonight in the forties. You're playing on the floor nearby, happy and content for the moment.

You've become belligerent about solid foods. Perhaps it's my timing. You'll eat only a few mouthfuls before closing your lips and growling at me, refusing to take any more.

You've discovered how to make a new sound. You pucker your lips and grunt. It resembles the throaty chant of a Tibetan monk.

You now respond to your name by turning your head, and you can understand certain words. For example, Lynne held her hand out to you after you'd fallen backward from a sitting position, and said, "Give me your hands." You grabbed her hand with both of yours.

Wonderful! I just felt you nudge my shoe and looked down to find you rocking on your hands and knees, the first "step" toward crawling. Maybe it won't be long, and you'll be mobile. The house awaits, baby proofed with all breakables out of reach and all outlets plugged with plastic.

12 May

The rocking you do on your knees and hands is growing ever closer to crawling. Occasionally, you'll push yourself into a squatting position if you have something sturdy before you to grip, looking a lot like a Japanese Sumo wrestler.

You started eating vegetables this past Sunday, beginning with carrots, which you like. You now eat cereal and fruit for breakfast and dinner, and a vegetable for lunch. Between meals, we supplement your diet with formula. The weather's become more seasonable, in the eighties, and your intake of water has increased accordingly.

Tomorrow night, Paula and Dana are scheduled to arrive. I'm interested in how you'll get on with them. In the coming months, I want to introduce you to other infants and toddlers so you can experience people your own size. We don't have any friends with children your age, so I'll have to seek out a toddler/parent group or begin one. If we don't adopt (a possibility Lynne and I have begun to discuss), you will have a solitary childhood ahead, but it doesn't have to be bad. You have parents concerned about your physical and mental development. Being an only child, though, you'll learn to depend on yourself more than you would if you had siblings, and you'll probably choose your friends more wisely.

As an only child, you'll become more creative in your play time, generating games in which you assume the roles of both hero and villain. You'll respect animals more because they will become your friends, substitutes for people. When I was growing up, I enjoyed the company of pets, especially Fritz, our German shepherd that proved loving and protective and loyal. He filled a lot of time, but he still wasn't a complete substitute for human companionship. That's where Lynne and I will come in.

I recall the first time I considered the utter aloneness of people. I was maybe seven or so, and I wondered if other people thought the same way I did, had the same kind of imagination I had, heard the same kinds of voices in their heads, dreamed the same dreams, saw the same colors, or if their reds looked more like my blues. And then I considered thoughts, how a person can *think* any thought with no one else knowing, how the *self* is concealed inside the skull, unable to experience another's joy, anger, or sorrow—unable to share feelings without diminishing them with words. No matter if we gather in crowds or shun others' company, we ultimately walk alone, Becca, through life and into death.

15 May

Paula and Dana have come and gone, and we've discovered that you aren't thrilled with strangers holding you or attempting to cuddle you. But once you grew accustomed to their presence, you allowed them to feed you and even keep you alone for a while. It was the first time since you were born that both Lynne and I were away from you simultaneously, and I found myself rushing to complete errands to get back home.

Paula brought news that blame for the situation between Elizabeth and us has been laid squarely on me and the infamous letter we sent to her. Paula said she's attempted to convince Elizabeth repeatedly to visit us with her, but Elizabeth has refused. I told Paula that we'd be happy for Elizabeth to visit, to act in a responsible and parental way, but, I said, "if Elizabeth plans to bring an attitude with her, I'd rather she stay away."

18 May

Well, kid, you had a long and restless night. You were sucking and gnawing on my finger for comfort at 4:20 a.m., then suddenly chomped down. Yow! A tooth's coming in, and we're all paying the price. You've bitched most of the day, gnawing relentlessly on frozen cloths, teething rings, toys, fingers, toes, but nothing works well enough to stop the pain. At the moment, you're on the bed, distracted from the irritation by struggling attempts to crawl. Thursday, you'll return to the doctor for another round of shots and your six-month checkup. Six months. It seems like six years and only yesterday. Lynne's hives have grown worse. (Could they be stress related? After all, they've grown worse with the new information about Elizabeth's continuing animosity.) She plans to query the doctor again later this week.

21 May

You're fifteen and a half pounds, twenty six and a half inches. You shed a few tears for the two shots you received today, but you took it all well enough. You're right on track in development—even ahead in some areas such as pulling up and standing on your own. Wonderful news. Your next appointment, barring any colds or accidents, will come at twelve months.

Lynne met us at the doctor's office, and afterward we all went to lunch, your first at a restaurant since starting mid-day solids. You did well, considering lunch edged into your nap time and you'd just come from a rather traumatic sticking of needles.

Lynne's birthday is only four days away, so today we bought a Ewan MacColl CD, which means we have more shopping to do for more appropriate presents. We want to do a good job on this birthday. Bouts of depression persist, so we must do our best to make her happy. (When Mom ain't happy, the saying goes, ain't nobody happy.)

Chapter Twelve

26 May

You, Lynne, and I spent a lazy yesterday together, a cloudy, cool day for Lynne's thirty-sixth birthday. We did a good job, Becca: We made her happy. Her depression evaporated for the day, and neither she nor I jumped to a fight. We both had a great time, playing on the floor with you, ogling for the camera, snoozing, reading, listening to music. Wish we could spend at least one day a week like that.

After several wonderful nights of sleeping through, you've begun to wake again, returning to old feeding habits. You're once again waking at least twice each night. And, again, certain friends and relatives have instructed us to let you cry, that "she'll learn." They're right too. You *would* learn. You'd learn that you couldn't count us when you needed us.

Perhaps you're "reverting," as the books call it, anxious about new experiences, wanting to continue the familiar. You now shun solid food, preferring formula. Too bad you can't simply talk to us, tell us what's bothering you. The inability to communicate readily and directly is the most difficult part. We have to guess at your needs, then hope we haven't guessed wrong.

29 May

You've had a wonderful day and are now sucking down your mid-afternoon formula after two hours of self-entertaining play, tossing toys, and bouncing and climbing on my leg as I worked. You even scooted forward today, the last step before actual crawling. Soon you'll be griping because gates will be blocking your access to other rooms.

You're still waking during the night, but you're feeding on solids better, especially now that the variety has expanded. We've added toddler biscuits and cookies, green beans, and a few other vegetables, all of which you like.

Your bottom two front teeth are coming in well which means the sucking and gnawing on our fingers has come to an end. Tomorrow, you and Lynne will do the grocery shopping while I clean house. That'll give me some time alone, albeit busy time. Ah, time alone. It's been a long while since I've had any. As an only child, you'll eventually require time alone, an opportunity to regroup, reflect, to keep your mind straight. I had planned some time alone for last Saturday while you and Lynne went clothes shopping, but a business associate of mine died earlier in the week, requiring attendance to his memorial service that morning. When I returned home, you and Lynne were already back.

Throughout the service, pictures of you and Lynne (you, poking your head over the bathtub rim; Lynne, repeating wedding vows, lying on the delivery table, playfully rolling on the floor with you) flashed repeatedly in my mind. No matter how happy or volatile relationships, they all end the same way, in ashes and dust. So fragile is our existence, and yet we expend such extreme energy mucking up our lives instead of relishing them.

When I arrived at the church, I entered through the rear door, saw about thirty people milling in the hall outside a small chapel room. I entered the room, assuming it would be the location for the service. After twenty minutes of watching people come and go, I finally figured out the room wasn't for the service, but to accommodate the deceased's immediate family until time to enter the main church for the service.

I'm not up on funeral protocol. At my grandfather's funeral a few years back, I arrived late, missing the entrance instructions. The family line had already formed and had begun to enter the church. My father, who led the procession, motioned for me to fall in line, which I did—directly behind him. What I didn't understand was that my grandfather's children were supposed to lead the line while his grandchildren and siblings brought up the rear. I then sat in the wrong pew and was asked to move—embarrassing. I hadn't seen most of the relatives in nearly twenty years. Another twenty will do just fine.

You're snoozing, and you didn't flinch when the phone rang. The state's business magazine's editor asked if I'd like to do an investigative article. You bet I would. Adult conversation, writing on assignment and not speculation—money! But I can't. The piece would require too much time developing contacts, too many interviews, too many spur-of-the-moment phone and out-of-home conversations. Spur-of-the-moment is a thing of the past. Your schedule decides how this household's run now. So I turned the piece down.

Lynne and I have discussed selling this house. Redstone Arsenal is slated for expansion as the Army consolidates several operations here, which means more opportunities and job security for her. We're considering buying land and building. We may put this house on the market by the end of summer. If we don't sell it soon, we'll have to replace eaves, siding, roof and garage door, and complete several other costly repairs not worth the investment.

We received a letter from Paula and Dana last week with pictures they took during their visit here. In the letter, Paula said she and Carol are planning to visit near the end of July, bringing Allen and Leigh with them. Good. We want you to know your young relatives, especially since there are so few of them.

30 May

You reached another first today, dear girl. You and I were on the floor in the living room; Lynne was in the kitchen. I had just turned on the audio recorder to capture your grunts and gurgles when you lifted yourself onto your knees and hands and crawled.

"She's crawling!" I shouted.

Lynne came into the doorway, nodding nonchalantly. "She crawled earlier," she said, "while you were in the shower."

Your progress was limited, mind you, only a couple of "steps," but you *did* crawl. Mobility! Can I count on increased self-entertainment now?

The mail carrier brought you a gift today, a "peek-a-boo" music box from Paula and Dana. The letter enclosed asked us to send them your Social Security number so they could purchase a savings bond in your name. You also received a "happy six-month birthday" card from Raissa, my elderly Russian pen friend with whom I've corresponded for nearly eight years.

Tomorrow, depending on the weather, we'll either venture up to Green Mountain for a walk around the pond or, if rainy, attempt to catch you crawling on video. Lynne continues to have bouts of depression coupled with the ever-present hives, and we both continue to be shorter tempered than before your birth, but we are edging back toward normal. If only normal would come a bit more quickly . . . .

It's 10:40 p.m. You and Lynne are asleep as I write. I've decided to stay up late to complete personal correspondence since Lynne will rise with you if you wake tonight. That's one of the good things about weekends: Lynne takes the night feedings. A friend whose daughter is age five suggested that you may be experiencing a growth spurt, causing you to wake more frequently, to eat ravenously some days and hardly anything on others, and to be crankier than usual. But do you have to do so much spurting at night?

4 June (5:00 p.m.)

You're sitting near the entertainment center, playing with wooden stirring spoons, plastic measuring spoons, some pots and a few toys. Lynne lies a few feet away from you with her feet propped on the couch. She's been off from work the last two days, taking new medication to fight hives that covered nearly eighty percent of her body. The medication has them under better control today, but it takes a toll, causing drowsiness. And she seems somewhat depressed, possibly an enhancing side-effect of the medication. The cause for the hives remains undetermined, which means more medication until the problem clears up on its own as it did for a short while during the pregnancy, or until the doctor discovers a cause through vast allergy testing. She plans to return to work tomorrow.

Although you now have the ability to crawl, you avoid it as much as possible, whining for us to lift and carry you. Look, kid, you have to do this on your own.

Lynne just scooped you up from the floor and carried you off to the bathroom for your bath. You'll have a great time splashing, but then you'll grow extremely grumpy from the end of the bath until around eight when you'll finally drop off to sleep. Last night, you woke only once, but you cried out in your sleep a couple of times. What demons haunt your dreams?

11 June

We're trying something different tonight—in fact, two *somethings* different. First, we're going shopping during the time when you're usually the grumpiest. Then, fools that we usually are, we plan to eat out in the hope that you'll be asleep by then.

As you mutter "buh, buh, buh" before the hearth while chewing on a *Pet the Bunny* book, you're in a good mood—so good, in fact, you've just put the book down and started crawling off toward the kitchen. Maybe you'll remain in a good mood throughout this overcast day.

The constant waking at night has taken its toll on our daytime energy, so we decided to try an alternative several of the parenting books suggest: a family bed. We now place you in your bed to begin with, but if you wake twice during the night, we bring you to bed with us. This week you've been extremely restless. You'll curl against me and begin to thrash, not fully awake, certainly not soundly asleep. While we still lose sleep, it isn't nearly as much as before. Most of the night after coming to bed with us, you remain peaceful and quiet, preferring to snuggle against me instead of lying in the middle of the bed where I place you repeatedly throughout the night.

We're counting blessings this week. You made it through a difficult delivery, a hell of a difficult first two weeks, and through the first six months, the most likely time for crib death. I didn't believe in miracles until I saw Lynne give birth to you. I'm thankful the miracle continues.

16 June

I rolled the computer into your room today. You're tugging at the printer's plastic cover on the cart's second shelf. At 9:30 this morning, a realty agent will stop by to discuss the possibility of handling the sale of our house. This past weekend . . . no, first I should tell you about your inaugural evening at a not-so-fast-food restaurant.

Simply put, you were wonderful. You sat patiently in the high-chair munching on crackers, eyes wide with fascination as you watched the people seated at other tables or flowing past you. Lynne and I were able to converse normally and to eat slowly and at the same time. Now, getting back to the weekend . . . .

Friday and Saturday went well enough, but Sunday and Monday found Lynne and me back where we were a few months ago during the more difficult period following your birth. We began looking at houses to get an idea of what was available to help us decide whether we wanted to buy land and build or buy a house already built. I don't know for sure what set us off—perhaps the cynical comments I made about living in certain areas—but Lynne and I ended up angry with each other. We finally talked through the anger yesterday afternoon, and all is well until the next series of misinterpretations occur. In fact, we've gotten to the point we each explain our statements—"I just meant . . . ." to avoid misunderstandings.

You've become an agile crawler with obstacles not as challenging as they were a week ago. For example, pillows on the floor last week proved impossible for you to negotiate, but now you're crawling easily over them. You still have accidents—an arm slipping from under you here, a loss of balance there. Sunday, a hand slipped out from under you, and you banged your head against the kitchen floor, raising a knot above your left eye. And a few days ago, your first bruise, on your left knee, showed up, the price for crawling across hard surfaces. But overall your coordination is improving by the hour.

22 June

I'm not sure what the new problem is between Lynne and me, or if it's the old problems reviving. She suggests our argumentative tendencies are due to exhaustion and the fact that we're still adjusting to the presence of another family member. I don't know, but, since your birth, we've seen sides of our personalities we did not know before existed, facets we detest. Minor differences flare into major arguments that end with one of us either walking out or shutting down, eventualities that never before occurred. Even our attempts to avoid arguments, explaining even the most innocent of comments, can erupt into challenges and accusations.

I admit I'm quicker to the fight. Lynne also acknowledges her decreased tolerance as she continues an ongoing battle with depression, but she adamantly dismisses any suggestion that the depression and her irritability could be due to hormonal imbalances. I suppose we'll work through this period of difficulty as we've worked through others in our relationship, but we always knew the cause before and dealt with it head-on. This time it's different.

You reached another "supposed to" Sunday. Holding toys in each hand, you banged the two together. And you're easily pulling into a standing position to take a couple of supported steps around the coffee table. All of your developments are so thrilling to watch. If our irritability is truly the result of our slow adjustment to your presence as Lynne suggests, perhaps it will be your presence that eventually solves our problems.

Bought your first cap yesterday, a tiny painter's cap, and you love it, jumping wildly and giggling when I put it on you. You haven't once tried to remove it. At the moment, though, you're in a grumpy mood, needing a nap, but you won't close your eyes, so I'll take you for a walk which usually lulls you to sleep when you're like this.

Your night waking continues, averaging two per night. We hope to gradually return you to your crib, beginning this weekend. Lynne and I at first disagreed about you sleeping in bed with us. She believed you should be left in your crib despite the number of times you woke each night, but now she's reluctant to send you back.

25 June

Gradual became immediate. Wednesday evening we placed you in your crib and not once throughout the night did you stir.

Lynne and I continue to discuss the problems between us, but we don't know exactly what those problems are. We agreed we must return to a system where we argue according to set rules—intelligent arguments that settle disagreements instead of resorting to childish, petty squabbles.

In high school we broke up once, then again in college. We've survived a few rocky times in our marriage as well, always able to work things through. In the past few weeks, I've sensed our relationship slipping into the way it became prior to each break-up, a certain distrust and even dislike for one another, but we have too much at stake now to give up easily. For one, we have all that history behind us. We've shared too many failures and victories to toss them aside without serious attempts at salvaging the relationship. For another, you are now a reality. You are the culmination of our relationship, a whole made from a piece of each of us. Lynne may have carried you in her womb for nine months, but for every kick and inconvenience she suffered or rejoiced in, I suffered and rejoiced as well. Although many women are quick to claim men are incapable of comprehending the burden of childbearing, men may in fact have a more difficult time than their mates. Men, unlike their mates, have no control in the process other than impregnation. They can't help the process, ease the pain, or protect when something goes wrong. They must watch helplessly as their mates endure the pain and joy alone. People who believe the mother is the only one who "suffers" during pregnancy and birth are imbeciles.

You accompanied me for a haircut yesterday, but it was an exercise with dual purpose. The stylist's teenage daughter entertained you while my hair was cut, and you had a great time. In the next couple of weeks, we will call on that girl to baby-sit while we go to dinner and a movie. We need the time alone together, to reacquaint ourselves with each other. It's time Lynne and I concentrated on getting our relationship back on track.

28 June

We had a great weekend, spending time together playing and talking, predicting what you'd be like. Perhaps we're beginning to work things out. Reading over prior entries, however, I see how you could easily infer that I'm blaming you in some way for the problems that exist between Lynne and me. Not at all. Whatever problems that exist between us are no fault of yours; sole responsibility lies with us and our inability to deal with changing situations.

You've learned to place objects into a container (blocks into a small bucket), and you can now play a crude form of patty-cake, slapping my upheld hands and giggling as I chant the rhyme. You've gotten stronger as well, easily pulling yourself up to negotiate from one end of the coffee table to the other.

7 July

Last Wednesday, you bit my finger. "Owww!" said I.

You pulled your mouth off, stared quizzically up at me for a long moment, then grinned. "Oww," you said. All day you repeated the sound, varying pronunciation from a rolling "Owwwww" to a long, playful "Oooooowowowow."

Thursday evening, Lynne and I left you at home with the hair stylist's daughter. She is sixteen and has an infant brother who she regularly takes care of—even through the night. You enjoyed her holding you until you realized we were leaving. She said you cried for a while after we left, then calmed to eat and play. She said you would regularly look around as if searching for us. We ate dinner at a Chinese restaurant, our topic of conversation centering on you and your development. We then went to a late show and returned home around midnight. Despite our conversation about you, it was good for us to get out together while leaving you in someone else's care. And it was good for you, helping you learn to function without us being present.

At the moment, you're vacillating between grumpiness and playfulness, entertaining yourself with the various toys strewn around the living room. Yesterday, we bought a wading pool for you, but the large Mickey Mouse in the bottom frightens you. You won't go near it.

8 July (2:45 p.m.)

I've been working on an outline for a new novel—
that is when you haven't been crying and complaining. The
living room floor is strewn with toys; so is your bedroom
floor. But you aren't interested in them; you desire only
what's in my hands, namely the computer keyboard. At this
very moment, you're trying to crawl over a pillow and several toys to reach me where I sit on the end of the couch typing. I didn't realize a kid your age could show such anger,
but when I thwart your efforts, your face grows fiery red as
you begin to cry and bitch. I thought mobility would help
you occupy your time better and curb your frustration. I was
wrong.

There. I've placed you near the fireplace with your
back to me. You're now banging on a toy xylophone. Uh-oh.
A glance around. You'll be on your way back any second
now. I'll close this down for the day and take care of a few
household tasks like vacuuming and dusting, activities that
always entertain you. By then, Lynne will be home to ride
the stationary bike, after which I'll feed you and she'll bathe
you. Here you come.

16 July (8:12 a.m.)

You're napping on the living room floor. You slept
through last night without waking after an extremely trying
day. Your appetite virtually vanished, and you refused most
solids and formula, even water, until late last night when
you accepted some formula. We suspect your front upper
teeth have begun to cut through.

I apologize, Becca, for not being the parent I should
be, especially lately as my temper has grown short. I've
become frustrated and angry because of the time required to
feed you and entertain you, as well as your persistent whining to be held. My anger is unjustified, and I must work on
better controlling my emotions. So how am I expressing the

anger if I'm not shouting at you or striking you? I bury it, clench my jaw, and do what I must do. And I write about it. Perhaps that anger even escapes in digs at Lynne.

Yesterday morning, you experienced the feel of rain on your face when we were caught in a thunderstorm in a grocery store's parking lot. You giggled and held your face toward the sky as the rain pelted down. In the truck though, the noise of the storm frightened you. I'm looking forward to the first rain shower you can play in.

Before you fell asleep a few minutes ago, I looked at your upper gum. One spot is red and tender where a tooth is about to break through.

You've had a great morning, and you're napping again. I forgot to mention that, along with your grumpiness yesterday, you suffered a nasty fall on the kitchen floor, face first, landing squarely on your cheekbone. The impact sounded like a roast dropped from about waist level to a concrete floor, but you're okay; not even a bruise.

I completed two poems this morning.

Dadhood (for Becca at seven months)

I'd hoped that, with mobility,
your dependence would grow less severe,
but you cling even more,
drawing yourself up, steadying
against my knees, crying
with hands held high, clawing.
So I'll play with you even more,
engage your mind and fingers
with blocks and squeaking toys,
then move away, slowly,
still poised to catch,
to cushion your falls.

Father's Day

The third and last card (on my first gift shop
       day as "Dad")
arrived late,
on the Wednesday following.
Of course, I'd done my duties, remembered
       my own father
with cynical lines mailed on time,
but I've never believed in that Sunday.

What of my daughter?
Will she choose the single day
to speak through Hallmark
or phone her cheerful wishes?
It comes down to role, doesn't it?
Titles and deeds and time.
Tests passed or ignored.

Please, give the day
to those who need it,
who require token thanks.
Toss the candy aside
and burn the cards.
Rewards earned
are never so fleeting.

21 July

Teething continues, but the pain is far less profound than last week when it had you too upset to eat well. Your appetite has returned, but the turkey mush you tried earlier didn't suit your palate. After tasting it myself, I understand why. Like paste. Today, part of your lunch came gushing back up as you gagged on a spoonful of that pasty mush. I then mixed the turkey with your applesauce, and you were able to swallow it better, but you still made a horrible face of disgust, not wanting to take it into your mouth.

Lynne and I are still swinging through those moods I've already bored you with. Lynne continues to believe the shifts are caused by our adjustment to you, but how long does it take to adjust? Until you're eighteen or twenty-one or thirty-five? It's just past noon, and you're near the entertainment center, playing with toys. I have set the computer up in a corner, wedged between the couch and front door, blocked away from you by the coffee table and a chair, which irritates the hell out of you because you can't get to the keyboard or the diskette boxes.

The cats fascinate you, but you ignore them occasionally in preference of toys that make comical noises. In fact, Leon at this moment is trying to get your attention by circling you and meowing, but you're too interested in an activity toy and its clicks and whistles and jingles. Uh-oh. Spoke too soon. You just grabbed a handful of back fur. Judging by the speed of his get-away, that's all the attention he needed.

Chapter Thirteen

30 July

Paula canceled her trip up this past weekend because her stepfather had to undergo tests to determine whether he had prostate cancer. Her mother, she decided, needed her close in case the news was bad, but the results came up negative. Carol, Jack and their kids, on the other hand, arrived on schedule.

Allen and Leigh were their typically unruly, undisciplined selves, which may have enhanced the fun you had playing with them, as you'll be able to see for yourself on video and in photographs. Unlike the time they came before your birth when we went sightseeing in Tennessee, we did little more than hang around the house and talk while you kids played inside and at the park nearby. Carol said that she and Paula might return in a couple of weeks since Paula is so eager to see you.

Your two upper front teeth have finally cut through. Others, lower and upper, have begun to come in as well. Irritable? You bet you are. Two nights ago, you and I spent most of the time in the rocking chair. You ended up lying on my chest from 3:00 a.m. until 5:00 a.m. as I tried to get some sleep on the couch.

We've listed our house with an agency and have begun searching for a new home in earnest. We've decided to buy an existing house instead of having a new one built. Building would entail two moves—one into an apartment, then another into the home months from now. We made an offer on a house and six acres last week, but the owner wanted to lock us into a contract while he continued taking bids without restriction, although he deemed our offer acceptable. We declined.

A few weeks ago, I mentioned that blood showed up in my father's urine, requiring a series of tests. Last week, the tests revealed kidney stones as the cause for the blood. Then he developed a large knot on his neck, so, yesterday, his doctor performed a biopsy with results expected in a week. As a precaution, the doctor also performed a bronchoscopy which revealed no sign of lung cancer, despite the fact that Dad's been a heavy smoker since his early teens.

When he called yesterday, Dad sounded like a man suddenly thankful for the years he's had and shaky with what might or might not be left, a man coming to grips with his mortality. The knot has him worried. "Lots of my friends," he said, "have died in the last few years just eat up with cancer." It's a horrible way for life to end. I've seen so many people waste away, grasping at hope and treatments that failed. One of my maternal uncles died of cancer which began in his lungs. By the time doctors diagnosed the disease, it was beyond treatment. He began to lose weight and ability quickly. Without medical hope, he turned to those television heal-a-deal preachers that always have their hands out. He sent them money, hoping to buy a prayer. He believed they would talk to God on his behalf, obtain a pardon, and he would rise from his bed for a few more years of life. But God apparently doesn't make deals with TV boys and girls. My uncle died at home in a room he did not leave for more than two months before his death. He had worked for the state's forestry department; he loved the outdoors, but not once did his family attempt to take him outside during those last weeks. If cancer withers my body, I hope I will have more than four walls and a television to stare at during my final hours. Let me feel the breeze on my face, hear the birds singing, see the sky. Let me shiver with the cold and sweat with the heat. Let me know life as I greet death.

When you aren't in pain from your teeth and your mood is good, you now explore more, venturing to your room on your own, or to the kitchen or to our bedroom. You plunder around, sometimes searching for the cats, then return to whatever room I'm in.

Lynne's hives continue. She's decided to consult a specialist unless they miraculously clear up before an upcoming appointment she's made.

(There you go, zipping off to your room again. I had to take a book from you because you began eating the paper. Don't believe you need that kind of roughage yet.)

A "fan" stopped by last week, an aspiring writer who'd read and enjoyed some of my work. He needed a stick-with-it pep talk. Glad to give it. He asked me to read one of his stories, and I enjoyed it, although, as I explained to him, it could be viewed as racist. It involves a black gay male cast in a not-so-favorable light. The writer cocked his head and grinned. "If anything," he said, "I thought it would be considered anti-gay."

I nodded, reconsidering the story line. "Yeah, I guess so," I said, "since gay bashing is in such vogue."

"I know," he replied. "I'm gay."

Prejudice and discrimination is a tricky art. Today, if you're white, racial prejudice is unacceptable, but prejudice against homosexuals is considered fine by some people. For other races, bigotry is not as readily condemned. We live in a society where nothing is absolute except our inability to treat each other with respect and dignity.

The variety of food you consume is growing. You now eat eggs, macaroni and cheese, and several meats, but the meat mush, like turkey and beef, is awful, so awful that you gag on it if it isn't mixed with applesauce.

You're crawling off toward the kitchen, pausing in the doorway to grin over your shoulder at me. You're babbling as you motor away now. Your vocabulary now includes bow-wow, mama, and dada, but you still haven't yet placed much meaning to any of those words.

Your balance has improved considerably in the last two weeks. You can now stand easily with as little support as my shirttail. My mother insists it's time to potty-train you because "Mama had you trained before you could walk." Maybe that's why I'm so anal retentive and compulsive. We'll train you when the time is right, when *you* indicate you're ready. One anal retentive person per household is enough.

3 August

We've made an offer on another house, a large, three-year-old home on a semi-rural half-acre lot. And someone is interested in our house but hasn't made an offer as yet.

Yesterday Lynne gave you your first taste of french fries as we ate lunch at a dine-outside burger shop. While I was at the window ordering, a man approached our table and sat down, but I wasn't aware he was there until I started back with the food. I quickened my steps. Around age fifty, unkempt, and reeking whiskey, he introduced himself as a "poor old Vietnam vet down on my luck. You got a dollar so I can get me a hamburger or something?"

"You want me to buy you a burger?"

"No," he said. "Just a dollar to help me get something."

"The mission," I said, "is only a couple of blocks away, and they serve lunch."

"You mean you won't give me no dollar?"

I shook my head, remained standing, ready if he tried anything.

He rose, began cursing softly.

"I think you should leave," I said. He became more agitated, his curses rising. I took a step toward him, and he began to back away. "I said you should leave now."

He started away, grumbling how "it ain't no way to treat a goddamn veteran." He crossed the street to sit on a curb with another fellow who handed to him a bottle in a paper bag. They were still there, drinking, when we left.

Could I have handled the situation better? Would giving him the dollar have made a difference in his life? Would it have bought off my conscience? I don't believe you can help someone who doesn't want to be helped. Giving people like him quarters or dollars only worsens the problem.

It's nearly 8:30 a.m., and you're napping. We'll soon go for a walk, then clean house before I get to work. I talked to Paula last night. She and Carol are still planning to visit this weekend. "And," she said, "I'm trying to talk Elizabeth into coming with me."

"Good luck," I replied.

4 August (11:00 a.m.)

Rain is pounding. You're playing by yourself near the front window, about four feet from where I sit on the floor at the coffee table. I wish I could get inside your head, know your thoughts and feelings more completely instead of having to guess at them. I hunger for the days when we can communicate.

The owners of the house we were interested in aren't willing to negotiate, but the realty agent continues to push. "The agent we bought this house through," I told him, "rushed us into buying something we weren't fully satisfied with. We won't be rushed this time. We made a fair offer. If they aren't interested, that's that." The realty agent then said he'd see if he could cut his commission to get the price down some. Lynne returns to the doctor today to begin blood analysis, the first step to uncovering the cause of her hives.

The rain's beginning to slack some. You've crossed the room and have begun bouncing against my shoulder, growling. Guess it's time for lunch.

5 August (11:00)

Talked with Paula last night. She invited Elizabeth to come with her to visit us this weekend, but Elizabeth refused, saying we owed her an apology for all the pain we've caused. Good grief. Is it impossible for the woman to admit she made a mistake? Does she feel she can't back down, can't be perceived as the victimizer, only the victim, no matter the cost?

Last night we ate out because the guy who's considering buying our house wanted his parents to take a look at it. According to the realty agent, all liked it, and an offer may come today.

You began a new food yesterday at the restaurant—pudding, which you apparently liked, although we can't be sure, especially in a public place because you eat anything placed before you if something more interesting has your attention. I've threatened to take you to restaurants for every meal so you'll eat without a fuss.

Last night from 11:00 p.m. until shortly past 1:00 a.m., I held you, first rocking you in the chair, then on my chest as I lay on the couch. Two more teeth are cutting through. After these, two more will probably follow quickly, but that should be all until you're around sixteen months old. By then, you'll be able to better cope with the pain.

Another call from Paula: Her and Carol's visit may be delayed. Carol may not be able to take Friday off as she'd expected.

You've fallen asleep on the floor with one leg draped over my thigh. Sweet dreams, Becca.

12 August

Paula and Carol canceled because Carol had to work. Turns out a good thing. We've signed a contract to sell our house, and we made another bid on the house we were interested in, reminding the realty agent of his offer to trim commission. The owners accepted. We've been packing household goods since then in preparation for a move that will come at the end of this month or early next. Moving will be a massive task with all that we've accumulated over the last six years. The house we're buying is much larger than this one. You'll have a big bedroom and a nicer neighborhood to grow up in, though the school system could use improvement. Paula said that maybe she and Dana would visit us in mid-September.

Your teeth continue to bother you as numbers five and six come in. The past couple of nights, I've sat and rocked you for hours on end. Lynne handles the weekend nights.

Lynne's hives remain a mystery, even to the specialist that examined her Monday. Although she began undergoing allergy tests, the specialist doubts they'll reveal much. Hives like hers, he told her, usually run their course in two years without a cause ever defining itself.

Soon you'll be in the large-size diaper. Most babies your age have been in them for some time already. You weigh about twenty pounds now.

We've packed a considerable amount of belongings, but there's much more to do. You should feel lucky you're as small and as young as you are. You won't have to do a thing except watch us grunt and sweat.

17 August

You now point at objects that interest you, and you wave at people. A couple of days ago, you waved at a frail, elderly gentleman staring into space as he ate his lunch at Arby's. He straightened, grinning, and waved back. He did not take his eyes off of you for the rest of the meal.

You've developed small sores on your knees that may be the result of insect bites. The location, however, suggests crawling is the cause. Right now, you're trying to get to my keyboard. I'm sitting on the floor at the coffee table which is jammed against the computer stand to prevent you from reaching the computer.

I spent most of yesterday afternoon at a building-supply store, searching out materials for a small rocking horse and a larger rocking llama I'll build for you. After two hours, I had what I needed. I'll cut and assemble the pieces this weekend, then do the finish work after we move.

Dad phoned Friday. Doctors removed the knot from his neck. They told him they were reasonably certain it was not malignant, but then a visiting specialist discovered a new problem using ultrasound to examine Dad's kidneys. What the first doctor had diagnosed as kidney stones may in fact be tumors. Dad returns for more tests this week. He's worried he'll lose the kidney or that the tumors are products of a malignancy that has spread throughout his body.

Lynne's hives continue unabated.

And now you've become cranky. Come here.

19 August

Last night you pointed at me and said "Dada," so I guess you have connected meaning to certain words after all.

I've been constantly up and down with you the last two nights, but you're in good spirits today, so maybe your teeth aren't bothering you as much. Want to take a nap?

The closings on the houses are drawing near, but we don't know the exact dates they'll occur yet. We probably won't be in the new house until September 7 or so.

You're chasing one of the cats down the hall, but he'll slip into the middle room to leave you angrily shaking the gate as he sits just out of reach on the other side.

24 August

This morning I got into an argument with the agent we're purchasing the new house through. It ended with him figuratively hanging up on me. Here's how it came about.

He called this morning to inform us that the "only thing" remaining before closing was underwriter approval on our loan, a fact we already knew because we've been in touch with the lender. He asked about the progress here, and I informed him we'd close on this house next Monday, that we needed to close on the house he's handling as quickly as possible to avoid excessive rent paid by us to our buyer and paid by the owners of the house we're buying to us.

"You have to pay rent?" he asked innocently.

"Yes," I replied. "It's standard."

"Not with us," he said. "With us, the seller gets a week free. *That's* standard."

I asked him why "standards" differ so much between agencies. I heard him catch his breath, then he said, "Hold on." A moment later, his brother, the owner of the agency, came on the line. His speech to me boiled down to "We've been in the business a long time, and we know if it isn't spelled out in the contract . . . ."

The original agent then came back on the line.

I said, "So the only the thing that lies between closing on the house is loan approval, like you said."

"Well, I don't believe that's the *only* thing," he said. "You know, we still have to get the lot surveyed."

"A few minutes ago, you told me all that remained was loan approval, and now you're telling me the property hasn't been surveyed. What else?"

"Well, there's the loan and survey and a couple of other things."

"Exactly what *other* things?"

"It might take up to a week."

"What *things*?"

He placed me abruptly on hold. His brother returned to the line, said that the loan approval, termite inspection and survey remained, that we could close possibly by Wednesday next week. I thanked him for the information, said that I would no longer work with his brother, the selling agent, that the agency would have to provide a different agent to represent the sellers to us. Buying and selling houses is such fun.

In the meantime, you're resting and eating better now that the two teeth that were bothering you have come in completely. Over the weekend, I cut out the pieces for your rocking horse and llama.

Dad underwent further kidney tests last week, and the "tumors" turned out to be stones and a benign cyst. To say the least, he's relieved.

26 August

Last night proved devilish for you. You cried each time I put you to bed. I ended up holding you most of the night, not getting more than four hours sleep total. Today, you're mood is volatile. No temperature. No other signs of illness. More teeth?

27 August

Hurricane Andrew slammed into South Florida and then New Orleans over the last few days and has now been down-graded to a tropical storm as it moves inland. It is spawning rain, tornado and wind problems across the Southeast, and Huntsville is no exception. Today, we have flash-flood and tornado watches in effect. Skies are overcast, but the rain has yet to reach us.

So, Becca, what do you think so far of being an only child? When I was seven, I was in the kitchen with Mom on a hot, sunny day. Next to the door leading onto the back porch sat an old china cabinet with a shallow bottom drawer stuffed with junk and Mom's contraceptive pills. As I watched her take one that day, I asked her if the pills were aspirin. "No," she said. "I take them so I won't have any more like you running around." I craved the company of siblings, and I wondered, if she didn't want "more like you running around," why hadn't she used those pills to prevent me?

Lynne and I have decided to have no more children biologically, not because we "don't want more like you running around," but because of physical limitations and age considerations. After all, you're the best thing our marriage has produced.

1 September

Lynne and I celebrate our fourteenth wedding anniversary tomorrow. It comes during a hectic week of house closings and moving. We closed on this house yesterday. We'll close Friday on the house we're buying. Yesterday, I had to take you out of the attorney's office several times because you grew bored and loud. We had hoped to secure a sitter for you this Friday, but none we know is available.

Blood tests to determine the cause of Lynne's hives have turned up a different problem, a possible thyroid condition. Other hormonal levels are slightly off as well, which suggests that her depression has been primarily physically based. But am I going to say, "I told you so"? I don't think so. She'll take corrective medication for the next thirty days, stop for thirty days, then return for another checkup. As for the hives, who knows?

Tomorrow you and I will schedule power and water hookups for our new home. Lynne's arranged vacation leave for all next week to move and settle into the new house.

3 September

I've already mentioned that you now wave to people, but did I include the fact you wave at the cats as well? And doors and cars and dogs . . . .

You're still teething, and your demeanor is meaner. Complaining, crying, sleeplessness, grumpiness, clinging.

Lynne and I ate steak sandwiches and drank a bottle of wine to celebrate our anniversary last night while you griped around on hands and knees, responding to none of our attempts to soothe. You slept better, though, waking only twice, but quickly going back to sleep. It would've been a good opportunity for us to consummate the fourteen years, but the wine had an extremely relaxing effect. We both went to sleep.

At this moment, you're in a good mood, sucking and gnawing on a frozen cloth.

2:45 p.m.

A few minutes ago, you made two more first accomplishments: You crawled under a piece of furniture, then you crawled onto a piece of furniture. The furniture was the coffee table. You were after the computer keyboard.

16 September

We're in. After a back-breaking week, we're in the new house, and you apparently like it as much as we do. It's quieter, more rural here with birds singing, bugs buzzing, distant cows lowing. Lynne and I, though, have been arguing over little things again, and once again we've had to "talk." When will these talks become unnecessary?

This house has a formal dining room, but we'll use it as an office/playroom. Right now, you're racing around, banging on toys, tossing blocks, and using my maternal great-grandmother's walking cane to bang on the wall.

You regularly clap your hands together now, and you're growing more vocal (as if you weren't already vocal enough), screaming your delight at play and your frustration when a task proves too difficult. Your crankiness comes and goes in a schizophrenic manner. And your night waking continues. I hear women brag about their babies sleeping through the night, never stirring, little angels as quiet as down. I wonder . . . .

It appears the first visitors to our new home will be Paula and Dana Barr. They'll come the last weekend of this month. In October, Carol and Jack plan to visit.

You have so much room here, Becca. When I was a kid, the houses I lived in were small and weren't equipped with an indoor bathroom. This one has two.

28 September

Yesterday, on your ten-month birthday, you took your first observed unassisted step, going from my legs to the coffee table. You could in fact be walking completely on your own now. You regularly buzz around behind the clothes hamper, but you haven't yet developed the confidence to let go. Lynne and I are trying to help you, encouraging you to walk between us, from one to the other.

Paula and Dana Barr arrived as promised, bringing you a crib toy that projects a sleepy-time image on the ceiling while playing "Brahms' Lullaby," only it makes you cry. They have filled far more than the role of potential guardians. They have in effect become your *grand*parents, showing more interest, love, and understanding than either of our mothers.

We're slowly getting the house into shape, but it's taking time. So far, we've capped the chimney with a rainguard, repaired walls, attempted to repair one toilet's plumbing, bursting the tank in the process (and the new one is apparently leaking, but I can't determine where as yet), erected a clothesline, done some minor landscaping, cleaned, removed a shower stall door. Next year, we'll lay wood flooring in the living room and hall.

I've completed the rocking horse and llama, and you like them both even though you're still too small to rock on them without assistance. The llama, large enough for me to ride, should last you until you grow too old and tired for rocking animals.

One of our cats spent the weekend at the vet's and is there now with possible surgery pending. Expected cost around $400, which is $400 more than we'd budgeted this month. The problem is a urinary blockage, some stones, and also an air pocket in her colon, all of which makes me feel guilty for the way I've treated her the past few days. When I caught her urinating on cushions and on the floor, I thought her problem was behavioral, her reaction to a new home. I tried to correct her through the typical punishment, putting her in the litter box or putting her outside (no, I didn't beat her), because she showed no signs of illness. She still played rough and tumble with the other cat, but the abnormal behavior continued until I took her to the vet who discovered the physical problems. That leaves me facing the same dilemma I occasionally face with you: How do I apologize?

Chapter Fourteen

6 October (7:56 a.m.)

You're still asleep, but later this morning, you and I will run some errands. As of late afternoon yesterday, we again have a working computer after the other jury-rigged piece of crap bit the dust last Thursday. It wouldn't boot, wouldn't do anything except beep, click, and generate strange color bars on the monitor. I took it to a computer-repair center where it booted and worked flawlessly for two days before quitting. The technician said the problem lay with the power supply or mother board, that he could better pinpoint the problem if he could run it continuously for two weeks. Otherwise, he suggested an upgrade, new power supply and new case, another unbudgeted expense, but, so far, it's an expense that's working wonderfully. "Oh, by the way," the repair technician said, "did you know the original machine was not FCC approved?" Why am I not surprised?

Carol and Jack are in Nashville after a short visit with us Sunday. They'll stop by again Wednesday evening on their way back to Pensacola. They brought you an early birthday gift, a rocking Dumbo. They also brought a new supply of hand-me-down clothes, many never worn and still with sales tags, that should take you through age two.

You, in the meantime, are getting ever closer to walking. You already walk as long as you hold onto something like one of our hands for support. And you love to babble various sounds. Your favorite sound currently is "dolie dolie." You've also learned to shake your head "no," already practicing for the dating game.

7 October

Jack and Carol left Nashville a day early, stopping by last night. You warmed up nicely to them, playing ball on the kitchen floor with Carol and allowing Jack to tickle you while you patted his hand.

Remember the agency problems with purchasing this home? The latest glitches include loss of check for payment of insurance from the attorney to the insurance company; and the loss of original papers we signed for the loan.

Yesterday and last night were not good for either you or me. You were grumpy all day, clinging like a Koala bear to a eucalyptus tree, and I had diarrhea all day and night. When your bowel movement came, it came with a great deal of strain after nearly two days without a movement. Bright blood speckled the stool, so Lynne and I called the doctor who said to observe you carefully over the next couple of days while increasing your liquid and fiber intake, that the blood was probably the result of superficial anal tears. Of course, getting more liquid and fiber into you is more easily suggested than accomplished. You refused breakfast this morning—applesauce and oatmeal with raisins—but you drank some six or so ounces of formula, more than usual. You're in a better mood, playing contentedly on the floor behind me.

Lynne begins her regularly scheduled vacation this weekend. Next Tuesday, we travel to Georgia for four days. On the last day of the month, we go to Birmingham where I will take part in a book signing at a local book store.

Yesterday while preparing your meals for today, I placed you in the backpack carrier where you could easily watch over my shoulder. After I washed my hands, you imitated the motions. Today, you're stuffing your large ball inside a plastic container, taking it out, placing the lid on, taking it off. Keep up the good work, kid.

8 October

Okay, so we're a worried about you. After not having a bowel movement yesterday, you had one this morning, and, again, blood speckled the stool, although not as much as Tuesday. I took you in for a check, but, rather than check you, the doctor verified that blood indeed speckled the stool. She prescribed a laxative and instructed me to take blot samples of your stool after it softens. Now, wait and worry . . . .

18 October

Severe constipation, apparently. Your test results were negative, no blood. But you're still having problems with constipation, so we're feeding you the equivalent of baby roughage, Maltsupex, which is a barley malt extract and non-addictive like laxatives.

The vacation went all right. You especially enjoyed the butterfly house. We stayed two days at Calloway Gardens, then went up to Atlanta, rented a room at a motel in a neighborhood where the attendant said jogging would not be a good idea, then went to Underground Atlanta. By the end of the day, Lynne had decided we shouldn't spend the night in the hotel room since it wasn't clean or safe enough, so we came home, arriving here about 11:00 p.m.

Last night, we attended the opening of a friend's art show. He has some intriguing work, but nothing we can afford to buy. Lynne says she senses something "frightful" in each piece. That frightful aspect is what draws me to the work.

Yesterday, you received your first bloody lip. Lynne was ironing clothes and you were constantly tugging at the iron's cord. To otherwise occupy you, she placed you in the clothes hamper. You stood, tipped it forward, and hit the floor face down, bam and blood. Yes, she felt responsible and guilty.

Lynne and I are doing better. We now have sex an average of one to two times a month (we're not burning up the sheets, but at least we're keeping them warm). In fact, I was running errands one day but had to return home to pick up a notebook I'd forgotten. You were taking your nap; Lynne was sweeping. I wrapped my arms around her from behind, nuzzled against her. "Remember when we used to make love in the afternoon?" She smiled. "Want to now?" That was the first spontaneous and best sex we've had since prior to the pregnancy.

Maybe we're both getting better. Maybe we are finally adapting.

You and Lynne are playing in your room now. You were up front until you began banging the stereo speaker against the wall.

I haven't mentioned it before because I thought it wouldn't last (like your bleeding, I thought it would go away), but I've developed some heavy anal bleeding over the last three weeks. I don't believe it's anything to worry about, but I'm going to have it checked anyway. At my age, I need to play it safe. I'll know more in a week. That's when our doctor will check me out.

20 October

In a month and seven days, you'll have completed your first year. What do you think so far? Too many changes too fast? Or not fast enough?

You slept well last night, far better than Sunday when I was up with you five times before 1:00 a.m., and then twice more after that, getting a total of four hours sleep in no more than forty-five-minute stretches. I suppose your teeth were bothering you. You've been chewing your right index finger like a teething ring, gnawing the skin off the first knuckle.

I've been reading more about night wakefulness, and we may begin giving you water when you wake instead of formula, as one book suggests. The theory goes, the water will eventually become useless to wake for. We'll see. Maybe if Lynne and I start getting more rest, we'll be less stressed and our relationship will improve even more than it has recently.

Trees are in full autumn dress, leaves quickly turning and falling off. The last couple of nights have dipped into the thirties, near record lows for this time of year. Recent winters have been mild. Lynne hopes this one proves colder with heavy snow. She wants to show you how to make snow angels.

22 October

Last night, you slept—yes!—from 9:00 p.m. until 5:00 a.m. And after Lynne left for work at 6:30 a.m., you slept another two hours. You're in better spirits today, despite your teething and drooling. Can we expect more long, restful nights? Or was this a fluke?

25 October

Okay, kid, you think it's a great joke or what?

Thursday, you pooped in your bath (oh, yes, and while I was videotaping you as well). Then, last night after bathing you, I dried you in my lap as usual. You stood, holding my shoulders as I toweled off your back, and this strange look came over your face. Suddenly I caught a grand movement in my lap while yellow rain splashed down.

Although Lynne and I are still slightly on edge, last night and today have gone wonderfully, like family time should. At this moment, you and she are playing on the floor here in the office as I get some work out of the way and type this message to you.

You helped us plant some ground-cover junipers yesterday. You tossed more dirt on yourself than into the holes, but you got the idea. You're progressing at a fitful pace—not a "sleepy" baby at all. You've begun experimenting with an ever increasing array of sounds, including clucking and sucking noises, and you string babble words together, punctuating them with certain inflections to indicate statements and questions. You've also learned the art of tantrums. You go limp and fall to the floor crying until you realize it won't get you what you want. You are a character— a beautiful, lovable character.

26 October

The mail carrier brought a postage-due package today, so I hurriedly dumped some coins out of your piggy bank onto your toy chest, rushed back to the mail truck with you and change in hand. We returned inside where I began sifting through the mail. A few minutes ago, you crawled back to your room and grew deathly quiet. When I checked on you, you were about to put a penny into your mouth. I had forgotten to put the change back into the bank and put the bank away. I didn't know how many coins I'd left loose, so I called our doctor to find out if coins in the system would harm you, but the nurse assured me that as long as the coin hadn't lodged in the esophagus ("And you would certainly know if it had."), it would pass easily through.

When I was age two or so, Mom used to dump coins on the bed for me to play with while she napped. One afternoon (one of those few early events I recall vividly), I put some pennies in my mouth and nearly aspirated one. It lodged momentarily before I was able to cough it up. Mom never knew, and I've never put coins in my mouth again.

Forgetting those coins today was inexcusable.

Time to close this entry. I'm off to have my butt prodded.

27 October

You're eleven months old today, and you're celebrating by refusing to eat breakfast. No use in trying to force you. You'll eat when you grow hungry enough.

Yesterday's rectal exam revealed a couple of anal fissures and some scar tissue—nothing serious, but, because I'm approaching age forty, the doctor needs a few more checks to be certain. Tomorrow I begin a cleansing fast and laxative program in preparation for a barium enema Thursday morning which will determine whether I have an intestinal cancerous growth. Lynne will take the day off from work to keep you.

And what if a growth is found? I don't know. When I met Lynne, our relationship became my focal point. She gave me reason to enjoy life, and she helped me define my career goals, supporting my efforts unquestioningly. Then we decided to have you, and you've become the center of our relationship, the greatest and most mysterious creation we can ever accomplish together. I crave to be a part of your life into adulthood, a friend, an ally, father, *and* daddy. I want you to know *me*, not *about* me, but, most of all, I want to know you. You are one of the two most amazing persons I have ever met.

30 October

"Okay," says the doctor, "you'll feel some discomfort as I pump in air." Discomfort was an understatement. Air pumped in; barium followed; then came twelve different X-ray pictures. Now the wait, at least a week, for details on whether I show signs of lower intestinal cancer. The entire process, from check-in to check-out, took only a couple of hours.

Lynne's making a sunflower "suit" for you to wear tomorrow, Halloween night—felt flower petals on a green sweat suit. You'll look cute. We'll spend the morning in Birmingham where I'll participate in a book-signing party.

It's drizzling today with more rain in the forecast for tomorrow. Such lovely weather helps brighten the mood. To say I'm anxious about the barium enema results would be as much understatement as saying the tests were uncomfortable. Lynne too is awaiting test results on her thyroid. Perhaps both will come back with good news.

During the discomfort, I distracted myself with recollections of the pregnancy, the difficulty Lynne had, the discomfort she suffered. The barium enema was nothing compared to that. And I recalled your birth, your first cries, the moment I took you in my arms, the neonatologist with his arm around my shoulders, his words a muddle in my ears as I carried you from delivery into the newborn nursery where you were weighed and measured and washed. And then you were back with Lynne in delivery. Such joy and admiration. I have never been happier nor more thankful than the moment they first placed you beside Lynne.

1 November

It's nearly 11:00 a.m. the day before the presidential election, and you and Lynne are asleep, Lynne in bed with a cold, you on a pallet on the floor behind me.

Tooth number seven has broken through on bottom. Yesterday morning, though, it wasn't your teeth that made you cry. Lynne brought you to bed with us around 6:00 a.m. after you woke. You began crawling around, slipped out of her grasp, and toppled off the end of the bed, scaring you (and us) more than hurting (knocked the wind out of you for a moment). You ended up with a tiny bruise near the base of your spine.

We spent Saturday morning at the bookstore in Birmingham, with me seated behind a long table with other authors. Lots of traffic, but little in sales. We were back home by late afternoon where Lynne dressed you in your flower costume, taking you to two houses to trick or treat while I remained home to hand out candy to the few kids that came by. You certainly looked cute in your costume. We gave you a taste of chocolate, and—yeah, that's right—you liked it . . . a lot! Next year, you'll have a better time since you should be able to belt out "Trick or Treat" yourself.

Your vocabulary now includes cat, dog, dad, and mom. You've also been experimenting with the sound "fff." After Lynne carved the pumpkin Friday night, she held you close so you could touch it. "Say pumpkin," she told you. "Pumpkin," I repeated. "Pumkeen," you said. You said it only once, an accident of sounds.

You'll be a year old in twenty-six days. Will you be walking by then?

2:28 p.m.

Just got a call from the doctor's office. The barium enema X-rays show that everything's fine inside. What a relief, kid. What a relief.

4 November

Lynne's over her cold, but now I've got it. Today's rainy with the temperature in the forties. You and I have to go out shortly to get milk and do the bank transfers, but you always enjoy the outings.

Your next scheduled big event is the twelve-month checkup. Then comes Thanksgiving and your birthday. What a year it's been.

9 November

It's shaping up to be another clinging, crying day for you. Teeth again? At the moment, you're occupying yourself with a Playskool beach bucket of three-dimensional plastic shapes. Makes nice rattling and banging sounds.

We cleaned house Saturday and went for a short hike on Monte Sano Mountain with you perched in the backpack carrier. You enjoyed the ride without a gripe.

Lynne will have Veteran's Day off this Wednesday. The next holiday will come in two weeks at Thanksgiving with you turning one year old the day after. So far, kiddo, you've been in good health except for that bout of constipation and anal tearing. You've luckily skirted the colds Lynne and I have suffered, developing into a sturdy kid after a shaky start. We're so thankful you have.

We suspect now that your night waking is due to nightmares because you begin crying before you fully wake, and you don't immediately recognize us. If you are prone to nightmares, you'll be keeping company with me. My most recent came Friday night when I woke myself by shouting "get out!"

In the dream, this house was somewhat different inside and located on my paternal grandparents' property. I had been in the attic, searching for a reason why the house's internal air felt so heavy, but I couldn't find anything. When I returned to my and Lynne's bedroom, I had to kick the door open. Someone, Lynne I think, was behind me, out of view. I stepped into the bedroom, and the atmosphere grew suddenly stifling, pressing in on all sides, muffling like cotton. A woman floated before me with dirty blond hair flowing over her shoulders. She was dressed in a silky nightgown yellowed by time. Her skin was ashen. Her face was my own. She hovered slightly above the floor, grinning wickedly before starting toward me. I screamed "get out!"—the words waking me. I rose and checked on you.

You are in one bad mood today. This entry so far has taken more than an hour because you've been clawing and crying, and you aren't interested in food or toys or anything except being held, but even then you whine. At the moment, I have you set up in your high chair beside me with toys on the tray. You're vacillating between contentment and crankiness.

10 November

You're sleeping; it's nearly 2:00 p.m., time to start your food preparation for tomorrow. After a bitterly rough day yesterday, you now sport a new tooth, but another looms beneath the skin. That means another terrible day for you in the near future. But today's been good, and you're enjoying some rest now.

12 November

Last night, you were buzzing around the house, using the clothes hamper to steady yourself as you walked. Lynne was making banana pudding. I knelt before you, gently drew the hamper away, and beckoned you to come to me. You took your first series of five or six steps into my arms, but you refused to repeat them. You need to build more confidence.

16 November

All right! You're walking on your own now. Last night as Lynne and I sat on the floor facing each other, you walked back and forth between us. We started at three feet, then gradually backed further away from each other. You negotiated the distance each time without falling.

Lynne and I have begun collecting crystal figurines for you. The first, which should arrive in about two months, is in celebration of your birthday, a small cake with a single candle on top. Since the pieces are rather expensive, you'll receive only one or two per year, probably at Christmas and your birthday or maybe on the special "Becca's day" we've decided to have between our birthdays in the spring.

You also received your second head bruise Saturday, compliments of daddy putz who knocked your right brow against the car door as I lowered you to place you in your car seat. Another apology made, but not understood.

We shopped for your birthday and Christmas gifts, buying you learning toys. Soon I'll be ordering special software that you can use on the computer. If nothing else, you'll enjoy banging on the keyboard since you're forever trying to get at it.

We've sent a package of trivial gifts (tins of popcorn; a greatest hits tape of 1967 songs) to Paula and Dana for their twenty-fifth wedding anniversary. We also included the following poem.

A Quarter Invested

A certain glance,
a roll of shoulders,
signals read by two as one.
Time, the smith of souls,
has fashioned a house of silver,
buttressed by foundations absolute:
respect, commitment, passion.
Two pillars, one roof.
Sanctuary. Home.

Christmas shopping time is here. Although money's a little tight right now, we haven't done much to curtail unnecessary spending, but, after the first of the year, it's back to frugality. And we're pretty good at that.

The year has flashed by; it has crept by. It's been an indescribable, incredible experience, one I would not have missed, one I would not want to experience again. Above all, though, I feel honored and fortunate to know you, Becca.

19 November

After three wonderful days of you entertaining yourself enough for me to get a large amount of work completed, you are in an extremely grumpy, clinging mood today, clawing at my leg, refusing food, rocking, or play. Perhaps it's that eighth tooth breaking through.

Yesterday, you puttered around the yard with increasing confidence in your ability to walk. One of the neighbors stopped by with her Shelty. Earlier in the day, you'd watched from inside as it played in our yard. You'd called to it and knocked against the window, trying to get it to come to you. When it ran out of view, you'd cry. But when you finally got the chance to pet it, you drew back, unsure but giggling.

24 November

In a couple of hours, you and I will meet Lynne at the doctor's office for your one-year checkup.

We've edited your first-year video to present. Only a few scenes remain to be added, specifically those from your birthday when you dive into your cupcake and we visit the Birmingham Zoo.

25 November

Well, kid, you're doing wonderfully, so says the doctor. To remind you how frail you were and how worried we were a year ago: You weighed six pounds, thirteen ounces, and measured nineteen and a half inches. Yesterday, you weighed in at twenty-two and a half pounds, and measured thirty and a half inches—tall and lean and beautiful.

In 1966, Lynne's father gave her a $25 U.S. Savings Bond, one of the few items she had to remind her of him after his death in 1972. Yesterday she cashed it at a value of $104, a hundred of which she used to buy four $25 bonds for you—her father's gift to you, she said. It's nice to receive, but you can achieve such greater satisfaction when giving to those who appreciate the gift and the act of giving. Some people give to garner accolades that ring false; they attempt to purchase affection. While that may work for a while, in the end it fails. See through the people who attempt to buy your affections, Becca, and recognize them for what they are. Don't be drawn into their sick dramas.

27 November (10:29 p.m.)

What a wondrous year you've given us, Becca. Every day we've changed, we've learned, we've grown. Each of us has come a long way. Lynne and I have had to adapt our relationship to accommodate three instead of two. We've had to relearn how to live, constantly reminding ourselves that your needs come before ours, but we still have a long way to go.

This morning, you didn't want to eat your breakfast when Lynne attempted to feed you, so she let you feed yourself, but nearly all of the food ended up on the chair and floor. As I cleaned the floor, you grabbed my hair with your gooey hands. I finished the floor and walked away. A few minutes later, Lynne presented me with a CD as a gift of thanks "for all you've done for Becca and me over the last year."

For all I've done.

The words embarrass me because I realize how inadequate I've been, how inadequate I remain. Certainly, I'm a better father than many, but I'm also worse than many more. I have so much to learn, and the more I learn the better life gets. And life *is* getting better. Lynne and I have improved our relationship. Our marriage is no longer in danger—if it ever was.

We've also become better at dealing with the reality of our relatives. We feel sorry for them, and we regret that responses have resulted in such strained relations, but our responsibility lies with you, not them. We continue to send pictures of you to Elizabeth and others who have severed their relationships with us in the hope that perhaps someday they'll reconcile while respecting our wishes and decisions as your parents. Perhaps the following poems will become nothing more than reminders of more childish times.

Learning

This girl doesn't understand
invisible walls, only the solid blocks
she stacks high, learning as subtly
as a mother's revenge.

In the kitchen, cookies bake and meat roasts
during the mythical season of family unity,
but grandmother's phone rings dead.
And yet this girl,

she flirts with
anyone, everyone,
too young to understand
the sarcasm of a Hallmark line.
She slides past the Huggies and kissies,
settles in the middle of the room,
eyes circling, ears attentive.

In the End

You can pack months,
even years,
into an envelope.
One photo or a dozen,
it's all the same.
Stuff in a life,
slip it into transit,
and, on the other end,
they'll talk about birth
and pain and betrayal,
and thumb through
lost generations
while life and death
arrive marked
Do Not Bend.

After breakfast, we served you a birthday cupcake. You grabbed it with both hands, squishing icing and smearing chocolate all over your face and chair, flicking it to the floor, shoving it up your nose. Lynne bathed you afterward while I water-blasted the highchair outside (in a forty-degree drizzle!), then we were off to the Birmingham zoo.

You thrilled in seeing all those animals in person. "What does the bear say?" Lynne asked as we stood before the brown bear exhibit. "Grrrrrr," you said. You roared at the elephants and rocked back and forth in the buggy, dancing to your own inner song as we went from animal area to animal area.

From the zoo, we returned home for the opening of your gifts—a "dress-me-up" Ernie doll; water toys; and a bang-a-ball set. Then to your bedroom for the marking of your height on a material growth chart Lynne made for you. Then came a bath and bed. You woke around 10:00 p.m. from what we believe was a nightmare. Lynne comforted you and, in the process, fell asleep herself. You're both sleeping soundly in our bed as I write.

While we were out, Paula and Dana phoned and sang "Happy Birthday" (in two-part disharmony) on the message machine.

11:17 p.m.

One year ago at this time, I sat writing in a hospital room as Lynne slept and nurses cared for you in the new-born nursery. The challenge that lay ahead unnerved me. I felt incompetent and overwhelmed, elated and blessed, completely drunk on an emotional roller-coaster. One year later, the feelings remain as intense as they were that night.

Today begins a new year and a whole new world as you grow more independent and confident in yourself and abilities. For Lynne and me, your birthday represents a kind of graduation. We made it through the first year—with extreme difficulty at times, complicated by worries and anxieties and external pressures that were unnecessary and born out of ignorance and misunderstanding, but we survived with our relationship intact and a healthy daughter to share our lives. We've endured some trying times, long nights, and days of worry over your health and our feelings of inadequacy. But life is getting better. Although final word hasn't come back on Lynne's thyroid problems, she has a firm handle on her hormones, improving her outlook dramatically, and my state of mind has improved along with hers. She and I finally realize we are the luckiest people in the world.

We will never be able to express in words the wonder and joy you embody, nor will words ever correctly describe the depth of our love for you. As you are limited in your abilities, we are limited in ours, but we are all growing, day by day. Be patient with us, Becca.

At the beginning of all of this, Andrew asked me, "Why have a child?" I couldn't answer his question then. I can't now.

I no longer feel I must.

Long life and joy, dearest Becca.

Happy first birthday.

C. STEPHEN FOUQUET is an author of poetry, fiction, and nonfiction. His work ranges from dark fantasy and literary fiction, to literary poetry, to scholarly articles and investigative news features. *Notes to My Becca* is his second published book. He earned his bachelor of arts in communication arts, journalism, from the University of West Florida in 1979. Fouquet lives in north Alabama with his wife and daughter and the family's two cats. The family is "expecting" again: They've been approved to adopt.